rk of Hungry Minds, Inc.

books in the U.S., please call our
800-762-2974. For reseller information,
ase call our Reseller Customer Service

on Data

uide to a happy, healthy pet/

rica

e Harrison/Close Encounters of the Furry Kind
5, 20

8, 66, 86, 96
7, 122, 123, 127

51, 52, 62, 68, 77

137, 139, 140, 144, 149, 150
.ife Photography: 9, 13, 18, **21**, 33, 34, 37,

.lis Production Department

Howell Book House
Hungry Minds, Inc.
909 Third Avenue
New York, NY 10022
www.hungryminds.com

For general information on Hungry Minc
Consumer Customer Service department
including discounts and premium sales, p
department at 800-434-3422.

Library of Congress Cataloging-in-Public;
Fraser, Jacqueline.
The American pit bull terrier: an owner's
Jacqueline Fraser.
    p. cm.
Includes bibliographical references.

ISBN: 0-87605-383-5

1. American pit bull terrier. I. Title.
SF429.A72F734 1995
636.7'55—dc20   95-21235
             CIP

Manufactured in the United States of Am
14 ' 13   12   11
Second edition

Series Director: Kira Sexton
Book design: Michele Laseau
Cover design: Mike Freeland
Photography Editor: Richard Fox
Illustration: Jeff Yesh
Photography:
  Front and back cover photos supplied by Jean
  Courtesy of the American Kennel Club:
  Joan Balzarini: 96
  Mary Bloom: 96, 136, 145
  Paulette Braun/Pets by Paulette: 11, 12,
  Dr. Ian Dunbar: 98, 101, 102, 111, 116,
  Dan Lyons: 96
  Cathy Merrithew: 129
  Sigrid Mirabella: 23, 31, 35, 42, 44, 47, 4
  Liz Palika: 133
  June Pasko: 24, 45, 64, 87
  Janice Raines: 132
  Ted Schiffman: 5, 7
  Judith Strom: 96, 107, 110, 128, 130, 13
  Kerrin Winter/Dale Churchill, Outdoor
    49, 54, 63, 65, 66, 90, 96, 97
Page creation by: Hungry Minds Indianap

Contents

Welcome

to the

World

of the

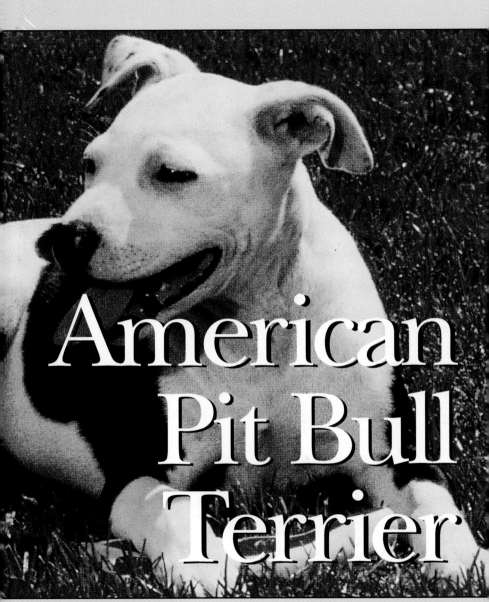

part one

American Pit Bull Terrier

External Features of the American Pit Bull Terrier

chapter 1

What
is an
American
Pit Bull Terrier?

The American Pit Bull Terrier is a fit and handsome medium-size dog with a muscular body, sleek coat, comical expressions and an affectionate nature. Considered the strongest dog in the world for its size, for many years it was one of the most respected and beloved breeds in our nation. A Pit Bull was the most decorated hero dog during World War I. Thomas Edison owned one. So did Teddy Roosevelt. "Pete," the Pit Bull star of the *Little Rascals* and *Our Gang* comedy series, proved the intelligence and adaptability of the breed by being the only animal actor to make the transition from

silent movies to talkies. But today, as you will see in chapter 2, this breed does not enjoy public appreciation as it did in the past. Before discussing the use, misuse and mislabeling this noble breed has endured, let's begin by clarifying exactly what an American Pit Bull Terrier looks like.

Every breed has a standard that thoroughly explains its appearance. Written by the national club that represents the breed, the standard is like a blueprint in words, describing how the ideal or perfect specimen of that breed would look. Reputable breeders think of the standard as an explanation of excellence and strive to produce animals that come as close to it as possible. Studying the breed standard is the best way to learn the distinguishing characteristics of a breed. The following is the standard of the American Pit Bull Terrier as approved by the United Kennel Club (UKC) in January 1978. The official standard is printed in italics, and explanations and comments are in regular type. Remember, the UKC standard explains only the breed's appearance. The breed's temperament is of far greater importance and will be discussed in chapters 2 and 3.

WHAT IS A BREED STANDARD?

A breed standard—a detailed description of an individual breed—is meant to portray the *ideal* specimen of that breed. This includes ideal structure, temperament, gait, type—all aspects of the dog. Because the standard describes an ideal specimen, it isn't based on any particular dog. It is a concept against which judges compare actual dogs and breeders strive to produce dogs. At a dog show, the dog that wins is the one that comes closest, in the judge's opinion, to the standard for its breed. Breed standards are written by the breed parent clubs, the national organizations formed to oversee the well-being of the breed. They are voted on and approved by the members of the parent clubs.

American Pit Bull Terrier Standard of the United Kennel Club

Head: *Medium length. Bricklike in shape. Skull flat and widest at the ears, with prominent cheeks free from wrinkles.*

The head gives the first impression of the dog. The skull is large and rather square, combining width and depth. The cheek muscles are well-defined, and the skin fits smoothly over the protruding muscle with no excess to droop or wrinkle. Through blocky and broad, the head's classic chiseled appearance, packed with bulging muscle, combines character with strength.

Muzzle: *Square, wide and deep. Well-pronounced jaws, displaying strength. Upper teeth should meet tightly over lower teeth, outside in front.*

The jaw should appear strong and bold with the underjaw very evident so the muzzle can end in an impression of squareness. This is just an impression. In reality, the angles converge a little and are not as square as those of the Boxer, for example. If the underjaw is weakly formed or receding, the muzzle will appear to be pointy in profile instead of square, and will also seem longer than it actually is. A weak muzzle lacks the characteristic look of power and is termed "snipy."

Sometimes a well-formed, squarish jaw is disguised because a dog has heavy, hanging upper lips. Pendulous upper lips hide the clean lines of the muzzle by falling below the lower jaw. Such lips were a distinct disadvantage in the warrior dogs of old and are still considered undesirable. The tighter the lips fit on an American Pit Bull Terrier, the better.

Many elements in proper proportion combine to give the Pit Bull its look.

When the upper front teeth meet tightly outside the lower front teeth, the dog has a scissors bite. It is the best gripping as well as the strongest bite, and is considered ideal. There are three types of less-than-perfect bites. One is the undershot mouth, where the lower jaw protrudes so that the lower front teeth (incisors) close in front of the upper incisors. Another is the overshot mouth, in which the upper jaw protrudes so there is a space or gap between the upper and lower incisors when the mouth is closed. More rare is the wry bite, a scissors bite on one side but undershot on the other side. Dogs with slightly faulty bites have no trouble eating. Most incorrect bites are a cosmetic fault, not a functional problem.

Ears: *Cropped or uncropped (not important). Should be set high on head, and be free from wrinkles.*

Cropped ears are trimmed in an attractive, prick-eared style. Uncropped ears are simply the natural ears with which the dog was born. Both cropped and natural ears should add to the American Pit Bull Terrier's animated expression by alerting to stimuli.

The most attractive natural ears are fairly small and are rose or half-prick. Rose ears have a backward fold allowing a bit of the burr (inner ear) to show. The tips of rose ears usually point toward the side, but they may also point toward the back of the dog's head, depending on their size, formation and whether or not the dog is responding to stimuli or resting. Generally the tips move forward and point sideways when the dog is alert and lie toward the back when the dog relaxes.

Half-pricked ears start upward and then fold over toward the front about halfway up. Sometimes the tips hang slightly to the sides of the dog's head, but they are always closer to the front than rose ears. Like rose ears, half-pricked ears also look nice when they are on the small side.

An occasional American Pit Bull Terrier has full drop ears of the type seen on retrievers and spaniels. Such ears are not typical of the breed and add nothing in the way of animation to a dog's expression, but function just as well as any other ear.

Eyes: *Round. Should be set far apart, low down on skull. Any color acceptable.*

Closely set eyes are a cosmetic fault that tends to make a dog look crafty and sly rather than intelligent. They also make the muzzle appear too narrow and too long, robbing the dog of the bold expression that is so much a part of this breed.

When the outside corner of the eye is in line with the indentation seen directly over the beginning of the cheek muscle, the eyes are set at the most attractive height in relation to the skull.

Nose: *Wide-open nostrils. Any color acceptable.*

Neck: *Muscular. Slightly arched. Tapering from shoulder to head. Free from looseness of skin.*

The neck should be well-muscled and appear strong. This is especially important along the top, where good musculature accentuates an attractively arched neck.

The neck should be narrowest just behind the ears and widen downward gradually to blend smoothly into the withers (top of the shoulders).

Clean lines and tightly fitting skin are desirable in the American Pit Bull Terrier. Wrinkles of loose skin under a dog's throat are termed "throatiness" or "having a dewlap" and are a cosmetic fault.

As you will see in the next chapter, the American Pit Bull Terrier was created to be a fighting dog. Today dog fighting is a crime, but, as its standard implies, the dog should still look like a capable canine gladiator.

This happy Pit Bull displays her muscular neck.

Many of today's cosmetic defects were functional faults in the days when dog fighting was in vogue, as they tended to hinder, or at least not help, a fighting dog. For example, a dog with loose skin in the area of the throat (a dewlap) was easier to grab in that vital area than a dog with tightly fitting skin.

Shoulders: *Strong and muscular, with wide, sloping shoulder blades.*

Good shoulder blades are wide and well-covered with muscle. "Sloping shoulder blades" means that the shoulder blade or scapula (the bone that connects the upper arm bone with the vertebrae) should have a very evident backward slope from its lower end (at the dog's upper arm) to its higher end (just in front of the withers). Shoulders with the proper slope are often termed "well laid back."

Shoulders lacking in layback are called straight or upright shoulders. They occur when the highest end of the shoulder blade is too far forward—too close to the dog's neck. The reason straight shoulders are undesirable is because they limit the forward reach of the dog's front legs, preventing him from having a smooth, effortless gait. They also make the neck appear short and coarse.

A long, well-angulated (properly sloping) blade, with muscle well distributed over the shoulder area, helps the dog have ample reach with his front legs and gives the dog attractive flowing lines.

Back: *Short and strong. Slightly sloping from withers to rump. Slightly arched at loins, which should be slightly tucked.*

An American Pit Bull Terrier with good proportions between length and height is a rather square dog. This means if you measure him from the point of the shoulder to the point of the buttock, and then from the withers to the ground, the two measurements should be close to the same. An overly long back makes a dog too long in proportion to his height, and the excess length usually shows up in the loin, giving the dog's back an aspect of weakness rather than strength.

The dog's topline (the top of the back from the withers to where the tail begins) should flow smoothly without wrinkles of loose skin or rolls of fat. The top-line should be slightly higher at the withers than at the rump, with a subtle arch just over the loin area.

THE AMERICAN KENNEL CLUB

Familiarly referred to as "the AKC," the American Kennel Club is a nonprofit organization devoted to the advancement of purebred dogs. The AKC maintains a registry of recognized breeds and adopts and enforces rules for dog events including shows, obedience trials, field trials, hunting tests, lure coursing, herding, earthdog trials, agility and the Canine Good Citizen program. It is a club of clubs, established in 1884 and composed, today, of over 500 autonomous dog clubs throughout the United States. Each club is represented by a delegate; the delegates make up the legislative body of the AKC, voting on rules and electing directors. The American Kennel Club maintains the Stud Book, the record of every dog ever registered with the AKC, and publishes a variety of materials on purebred dogs, including a monthly magazine, books and numerous educational pamphlets. For more information, contact the AKC at the address listed in Chapter 13, "Resources," and look for the names of their publications in Chapter 12, "Recommended Reading."

There are several types of topline faults which in a mild form are mainly cosmetic, but if extremely pronounced are structural problems that weaken the back and can impede proper gait. One of the most common is a sagging (concave) appearance behind the withers as seen on a sway-backed horse. This is called a soft topline or a dip in the topline. Another frequent topline fault is roach back, a spine that arches in a convex curve that begins behind the withers and becomes extremely pronounced above the loin area. The withers should be the highest point on the dog's back, so a dog who is higher in the croup than at the withers is also faulty. This rather common topline problem is termed "high in the rear."

The loin area is the dog's waistline and should have a noticeable indentation when seen from above. It should not be so slim, however, that it makes the dog appear weak. The indentation should be just enough to give the body shape, so it does not look like a log or a plump sausage.

Chest: *Deep, but not too broad, with wide-sprung ribs.*

The American Pit Bull Terrier should have enough space between her front legs to make room for a well-developed forechest (also called the brisket). The forechest is the front part of the dog's chest. As it goes down between the front legs to meet the chest, the forechest should be deep enough at its lowest point to

The Pit Bull should look strong and fit—not weak nor flabby.

be even with the dog's elbow when viewed from the side. This does not mean that wider is better with regard to the space between a dog's front legs or the width of the forechest. An overly broad front is coarse and bulldogish, making for a less agile animal. No feature of the dog should dominate her other features. In the most attractive Pit Bulls, every part is in perfect proportion to every other part. This results in a balanced, athletic animal.

A dog with wide-sprung ribs appears well-rounded, not flat along the sides, a fault known as slab-sided. The Pit Bull needs a large, strong rib cage because it is the housing that protects the heart and lungs.

Ribs: *Close. Well-sprung, with deep-back ribs.*

When a Pit Bull's well-sprung rib cage continues far back toward the dog's rear quarters, the back is considered "well-ribbed," or "deep in the rear." This is important because deep-back ribs allow more room for lung expansion during exercise, giving the dog more physical staying power. A dog is lacking in depth of rib if there is room for more than the width of a hand between the dog's last rib and its thigh.

Tail: *Short in comparison to size. Set low and tapering to a fine point. Not carried over back. Bobbed tail not acceptable.*

The tail is important because it is a continuation of the spinal column. A tail that is noticeably thin and weak, or a kinked or crooked tail, could indicate a similar defect in the spine.

Pit Bulls were developed for optimal strength.

The ideal tail for an American Pit Bull Terrier resembles an old-fashioned pump handle. It should begin with a strong, thick root and taper to a point that ends even with, or a little above, the hock joint. The set on of the tail (where the root emerges from the dog's body) should be rather low, although not as low as the tail set of some racing breeds.

When the Pit Bull is moving, her tail should not be carried any higher than the top of her back. Tails that are held high above the back or that curl over the back are considered faulty. Some dogs hold their tails correctly most of the time,

but raise them higher than the standard demands when they are extremely excited.

A bobbed (surgically removed) tail (such as seen on the Boxer or the Doberman Pinscher) is not typical of this breed. The American Pit Bull Terrier should sport the tail with which she was born.

Legs: *Large, round-boned, with straight, upright pasterns, reasonably strong. Feet to be of medium size. Gait should be light and springy. No rolling or pacing.*

The leg bones should be large enough in circumference to appear to support the weight of the dog easily. A Pit Bull who resembles a log held up by toothpicks is both structurally weak and unattractive.

The Pit Bull's front legs should be straight and sturdy. The feet

Any color is acceptable for your Pit Bull.

should point directly to the front, not toward each other (toed in) or away from each other (east-west front). The lowest part of the front leg, from the joint just above the foot down to the foot, is called the pastern. It should stand erect and appear strong. If the front feet are at either a forward or an outward angle when they meet the ground, the dog may have weak pasterns.

Feet should never stand out as being either too large or too tiny for the dog. The standard simply calls for feet that are the right size to fit the animal. Other foot faults that could impede movement and stamina are flat feet and splayed feet (space between the toes).

The Pit Bull's gait should appear effortless. The dog should move forward boldly, with a jaunty, self-confident attitude and no wasted motion. When the dog trots, his topline should move smoothly. If it rolls from side to side, the dog's gait is not ideal. Many puppies roll when they are young and loose, but improve as their bodies mature and tighten. Also, some dogs roll because they are too fat or lack exercise.

When the dog's front and rear legs on the same side move forward together, the dog is pacing. While some dogs pace when they are tired, other dogs pace due to structural faults. The correct gait for the Pit Bull is the trot. It is a diagonal gait with the left front and the right rear legs moving forward together, followed by the right front and the left rear.

Thigh: *Long, with muscles developed. Hocks down and straight.*

The rear leg has an upper thigh and a lower thigh, separated by the stifle (knee joint), located on the frontal portion of the dog's hind leg. Both thighs should appear strong and be covered by hard muscle.

The hock joint is the joint between the stifle and the foot. "Hocks down" means that the hock should be located much lower than the middle of the dog's rear leg, rather close to the ground.

When watched from the rear, the dog's back legs should appear parallel. Hocks turning either toward each other or away from each other are faulty.

Coat: *Glossy. Short and stiff to the touch.*

A dog's coat gives evidence of the general health of the dog, and a Pit Bull in good condition usually has a beautiful, shiny coat. The hair should be rather coarse in texture, which provides the best protection in a short coat.

Color: *Any color or marking permissible.*

Weight: *Not important. Females preferred from 30 to 50 pounds. Males from 35 to 60 pounds.*

The Pit Bull's height and weight should be in proportion.

American Dog Breeders Association Standard

The American Dog Breeders Association (ADBA) also offers a standard for the American Pit Bull Terrier. It needs no elaboration, as the explanation of each item in the standard is part of the document. To obtain a copy of the ADBA standard, write to the American Dog Breeders Association, Inc., Box 1771, Salt Lake City, UT 84110.

The American Pit Bull Terrier's Ancestry

Archaeologists agree that dogs were the first animals domesticated by man. Cave drawings from the Paleolithic era, the earliest part of the Old World Stone Age (50,000 years ago), show men and dogs hunting together. Gradually, man found additional uses for dogs. The earliest known ancestors of the American Pit Bull Terrier served as guards and draft animals, but they were especially esteemed as dogs of war.

Origin of the Pit Bull

The ancient Greeks had huge, ferocious dogs of a type called Mollossian, which historians believe originated in Asia. During the sixth century B.C., Phoenician traders brought some of these Greek guard dogs to England. There they flourished and became the ancestors of England's early Mastiff-type dogs.

16

When the Roman Legions invaded Britain, they were met on the beaches by the Britons' fierce Mastiff-type war dogs fighting side by side with their owners. The Romans admired these fighting dogs so much that they sent many of them home to Italy. There the dogs were called Pugnaces, or the broad-mouthed dogs of Britain. As the Roman legions spread across Europe, so did the dogs.

Warrior dogs also starred in the bloody Roman circuses, where they were used to fight savage animals of other species, armed men and each other. Around 395 A.D., the Roman historian Symmachus wrote about seven Irish Bulldogs who excited a circus audience with their savage fighting and brave attitude. Symmachus called the deadly dogs Bulldogs, because dogs of that type were used to fight bulls.

The Ancient Bulldog

During ancient times there were no breeds as we know breeds today, and dogs were usually named for the work they did. For example, in England all guard dogs of massive size were considered Mastiffs, and all dogs quick, brave and small enough to enter a hole in the ground (terra) after wild game, such as badgers or foxes, were called Terriers.

Eventually, some of the Mastiff-type dogs became specialists. A 1632 dictionary defined the Alaunt as a Mastiff-like dog used by the British butchers to round up and pen fierce oxen. The Bandog was any large guard dog who was kept chained by day. And the Bulldog, of course, was the gladiator.

George R. Jesse, the famed British canine historian, wrote that the Bulldog was the result of selectively breeding Mastiffs to produce a smaller, more agile dog with a recessed nose and a protruding jaw. This, Jesse contended, would enable the dog to breathe freely while holding onto a bull.

The fearless, ferocious Bulldogs who were used to fight bulls and bears long ago were different from today's sophisticated sourmugs in both appearance and attitude. Ancient Bulldogs were taller and more agile, with nearly straight front legs, and they had longer muzzles than modern Bulldogs. Some even had fairly long, straight tails.

The Blood Sports

Blood sports were so much a part of daily life in England that around 1800, in the town of Wednesbury in Staffordshire County, church bells rang in celebra-

The Pit Bull is still a high-energy dog.

tion of "old Sal," when she finally managed to have puppies. Sal was famous for gameness but had never been able to whelp a litter. If a Bulldog bitch died during whelping in that mining district, women often raised the puppies by suckling them at their own breasts.

Bullbaiting and other blood sports were not just entertainment for the working classes. In fact, kings and queens often mandated that a contest be arranged. When French ambassadors visited the court of Queen Elizabeth in 1559, the Queen graciously entertained them with a fine dinner followed by an exhibition of dogs baiting bulls and bears.

King James I continued Queen Elizabeth's tradition by having a special baiting arranged to entertain ambassadors from the Spanish Court. His son, King Charles I, was also an avid spectator of blood sports, and during the days of Queen Anne (1665–1714), such spectacles continued to flourish.

Bullbaiting: Before a baiting, the bull was prepared in a prescribed manner. Either a heavy rope was tied around its horns or a wide leather collar was buckled around its neck. A stake was driven into the ground, and a large iron ring, acting as a swivel, was connected to it. Then one end of a heavy chain or rope was attached to the ring and the other end was fastened to the bull.

When a dog was released, he was expected to pin the bull by attacking it from the front and gripping its tender nose. Sometimes two or more dogs were released at the same time. Most bulls were tortured for hours in this manner before they were either killed by the dogs or slaughtered for meat, but an occasional bull became famous for its ability to defend itself and was used over and over.

For Bulldog owners, baiting was a compelling competitive event. They paid an entry fee for their dog to have a turn at the bull, and the owner of the dog who managed to pin the bull won a prize. During a baiting, bulls often tossed dogs 30 or more feet into the air. Meanwhile, owners scrambled to line themselves up below their plummeting dog, as they hoped to break his fall by catching him on their own shoulders. Men sometimes got too close to the maddened bull and were also tossed. Dogs who were so deeply gored that their organs hung out were still urged by their owners to continue the assault, and many dauntless dogs were trampled under the bull's hoofs.

Bearbaiting: Bearbaiting was similar to bullbaiting except that the bear's weapons were teeth and claws instead of horns and hoofs. Reports before the sixteenth century describe the bear wearing a collar and fastened to a ring and stake in the same manner as the bull. Later writings refer to a ring in the bear's nose.

WHERE DID DOGS COME FROM?

It can be argued that dogs were right there at man's side from the beginning of time. As soon as human beings began to document their existence, the dog was among their drawings and inscriptions. Dogs were not just friends, they served a purpose: There were dogs to hunt birds, pull sleds, herd sheep, burrow after rats—even sit in laps! What your dog was originally bred to do influences the way it behaves. The American Kennel Club recognizes over 140 breeds, and there are hundreds more distinct breeds around the world. To make sense of the breeds, they are grouped according to their size or function. The AKC has seven groups:

1) Sporting, 2) Working,
3) Herding, 4) Hounds,
5) Terriers, 6) Toys,
7) Nonsporting

Can you name a breed from each group? Here's some help: (1) Golden Retriever; (2) Doberman Pinscher; (3) Collie; (4) Beagle; (5) Scottish Terrier; (6) Maltese; and (7) Dalmatian. All modern domestic dogs (*Canis familiaris*) are related, however different they look, and are all descended from *Canis lupus*, the gray wolf.

Like exceptional bulls, an occasional bear became famous for its ferocity and fighting ability. Sackerson, a particularly savage specimen, was mentioned by Shakespeare in *The Merry Wives of Windsor.*

Dogfights: England passed the Humane Acts in 1835, making blood sports illegal. Although dogfighting was popular before then, it was often just one part of a full day of blood sports, a kind of warm-up before the main event. Interest in dogfighting grew rapidly after blood sports were abolished because, unlike bullbaiting rings, dogfighting pits did not require much space. Contests could be secretly held in cellars and the back rooms of pubs.

As dogfighting's popularity soared, the contests became more organized. Fight rules were written and

upheld, and handlers developed conditioning programs (keeps) for their dogs in an effort to have them reach optimum fighting weight just prior to a match. A dog was said to be at her best fighting weight when she carried as few pounds as possible while maintaining her full strength. Much more than pride was involved in the desire to win: betting was heavy and purses were large.

*An example of
a Bull-and-
Terrier dog.*

The Bull-and-Terrier

During the early 1800s, some Bulldog breeders tried something new, hoping to breed faster, fiercer fighters. They bred the most formidable baiting and fighting Bulldogs with the toughest, quickest, and bravest terriers. This cross was believed to enhance the fighting ability of the Bulldog by reducing his size while maintaining his strength and increasing his speed and agility. Although some historians say the smooth-coated Black-and-Tan and the White English Terrier (now extinct) were most frequently crossed with Bulldogs, others say the Terriers were chosen only on the basis of gameness and working ability, and that a variety of Terrier-like dogs were used. The result of these crosses was called the Bull-and-Terrier or the Half-and-Half. As time passed and Bull-and-Terriers were selectively bred, they became recognizable as an emerging breed.

An early Bull-and-Terrier named Trusty was so famous in England that an article and picture of him appeared in an 1806 edition of *The Sporting Magazine*. The picture is the first one known of a Bull-and-Terrier cross. Trusty was "as renowned for his battles as Bonaparte," according to the article, and "fought 104 battles and was never beat." Raised by a prizefighter and later owned by a succession of boxers, Trusty was eventually purchased by Lord Camelford and came to be known as Lord Camelford's dog. Later his Lordship changed the dog's name to Belcher and presented him to fighting Jim Belcher, boxing champion of England. His Lordship explained that "the only unconquered man was the only fit master for the only unconquered dog."

Arrival in America

Blood sports were popular in America, too, and the first Bulldogs and Bull-and-Terriers imported to the New World were brought over for that purpose. While bearbaiting was banned in New England as early as the 1600s, public spectacles such as bullbaiting, rat-killing competitions for dogs, dogfighting and cockfighting were extremely popular in New York City during the late seventeenth and early eighteenth centuries. Nearly all of America's early fighting dogs were British or Irish imports bred

In America, the dogs were bred to be bigger and stronger.

for generations to do battle, and many of the Americans who imported them continued breeding them for the same purpose.

Dogfighting was so accepted in America that in 1881, when a fight was held in Louisville between the famed

English imports, Lloyd's Pilot, owned by "Cockney Charlie" Lloyd, and Crib, owned by Louis Kreiger, the Ohio and Mississippi Railroad advertised special excursion fares to the big battle. Upon arrival in Louisville, bettors and spectators were taken to a fine hotel where they were warmly welcomed by the president of the Louisville board of aldermen, the police chief and other local officials. The referee for the fight was William Harding, sports editor of *The Police Gazette*, and owner-publisher Richard K. Fox served as stakeholder. Pilot and Crib each weighed in at just under 28 pounds, and thrilled the spectators by fighting gamely for an hour and 25 minutes before *Pilot* won the victory.

"Cockney Charlie" Lloyd imported other dogs who gained fame fighting in America and were also used for breeding. Among them were Lloyd's Paddy, Pat and Rafferty. In fact, some of today's American Pit Bull Terrier owners can still trace their dog's ancestors back to several strains of superior fighting dogs who arrived in America during the 1800s. A few of these strains are Corvino, Delihant, Farmer, Feeley and Tudor from England; and Colby, Corcoran, Gas House, Lightner, Noonan and Semmes from Ireland. The designation "Old Family," still in use today, refers to the Irish dogs.

AMERICANIZATION OF THE BREED

Pilot and Crib, two of the most famous dogs of their period, weighed under 28 pounds, yet the weight of a male Pit Bull today ranges from 40 to 65 pounds. What happened? Pilot and Crib were at fighting weight, but though they would normally have weighed several pounds more, it would not have been nearly enough to make up the difference.

One explanation is that because Americans always seem to believe bigger is better, they selected bigger dogs for breeding and thereby created a larger animal. Although this theory is partly correct, there is more to the story.

It is believed that the breed's general usefulness on the frontier was a factor in increasing its size. The

American pioneers discovered the Bull-and-Terrier's versatility, bravery and devotion, and soon the dogs traveled west, becoming indispensable members of many ranch and farm families. The dogs were well-suited to life on the frontier, and guarded homesteads and children with confidence and authority. Many of them also helped round up stock.

In addition, they protected the farm animals from predators and varmints ranging from rats and snakes to coyotes and bears. Eventually, the settlers probably decided that a slightly larger dog, with the same body style and bravery, would have an even better chance of defending the stock against marauding mountain lions and ravaging wolves. Consequently, when selecting breeding partners for their dogs, they chose larger specimens. For a more complete picture of the role of the American Pit Bull Terrier as America moved westward, read Marjorie Kinnan Rawlings' book, *The Yearling.*

The strength of a Pit Bull cannot be doubted.

Whereas few pioneers kept breeding records on their dogs, American dogfighters painstakingly cataloged pedigrees of their breeding stock. In fact they kept pedigrees (either in files or by memory) for generations. Many of them registered their dogs in 1898 when Chauncy Z. Bennett founded the United Kennel Club (UKC) with the American (Pit) Bull Terrier as its first recognized breed. Bennett created that breed name to help establish the dogs as an American breed.

The American Dog Breeders Association (ADBA) was created in 1909 by its first president, Guy McCord, and his close friend, John P. Colby. While some American Pit Bull Terrier breeders chose one organization or the other when registering their dogs, others listed their stock with both registries, and many still do.

The Dog of the Day

Every dog does not have his day, but the Pit Bull certainly did. His day was just before and during World War I, when he was so highly regarded that he represented the U.S. on a World War I poster depicting each of the Allied forces as a gallant dog native to his country. During that time, many issues of *Life* magazine featured political cartoons with Pit Bulls as the main characters. Pit Bulls even graced the covers of *Life* on February 4, 1915, and again on March 24, 1917.

Today, Pit Bulls are popular therapy dogs.

The first picture, captioned "The Morning After," showed a bandaged and scarred Pit Bull; the later one,

captioned "After Six," displayed a gentlemanly Pit Bull in a bow tie and top hat. Both were drawn by Will Rannells.

During World War I, the breed proved deserving of its country's esteem. A Pit Bull named Stubby was the war's most outstanding canine soldier. He earned the rank of sergeant, was mentioned in official dispatches and earned two medals, one for warning of a gas attack and the other for holding a German spy at Chemin des Dames until American troops arrived.

Following the war, the Pit Bull's popularity continued to grow. Depending on what it was used for and where it lived, the breed was still known by many different names, such as Bulldog, American Bull Terrier, Brindle Bull Dog, Yankee Terrier, Pit Dog, and, of course, American Pit Bull Terrier.

The first Pit Bull movie star was whelped on September 6, 1929. Pete, a brindle and white bred by A. A. Keller, achieved fame on stage and screen as the dog actor in the *Little Rascals* and the *Our Gang* comedy series. Owned and trained by Harry Lucenay, Pete's UKC registered name was Lucenay's Peter.

During the mid 1970s, both American Pit Bull Terrier registries, the UKC and the ADBA, began sanctioning shows for the breed. Since then, the number of American Pit Bull Terriers entered in shows has grown steadily.

Media Monster

As the years went by, pockets of underground dogfighting activity continued in the United States. By the late 1960s, some dog lovers were determined to put a stop to it, and in 1970 the American Dog Owner's Association (ADOA) was established for the purpose of terminating dogfighting.

The ADOA was instrumental in getting the Animal Welfare Act revised, leading to the arrest of many dogfighters. Meanwhile, the media focused its cameras and commentary on the teeth and muscles of the bloodied, exhausted dogs picked up during police raids on dogfights, instead of on the people who placed those dogs in the pit and wagered on the outcome. A media monster was born and its name was Pit Bull.

The Monster-Mobster Connection: Monsters are exciting. Children like to dress up like Jason, Freddie, Frankenstein and Dracula on Halloween; it's fun to pretend to be bad for one night. But the headlines and TV stories concocted about the Pit Bull attracted the type of people who weren't pretending. When the media manufactured a "bad dog" monster, young toughs, those who reveled in flaunting their badness, believed that swaggering through their turf with a Pit Bull by their side would enhance their image. When thugs heard stories about teeth that locked and incredible jaw pressure, they not only believed them, but exaggerated them when they bragged. Soon drug dealers, gang members and other hoodlums all wanted such a dog. Biologists eventually proved these theories ridiculous, but the punks read headlines, not academic reports. Thus the same breed of dog that laid its life on the line for its dogfighter owners became the preferred mascot of minor mobsters.

FAMOUS OWNERS OF THE AMERICAN PIT BULL TERRIER

Fred Astaire

James Caan

Jack Dempsey

Thomas Edison

Michael J. Fox

Helen Keller

President Theodore Roosevelt

Sir Walter Scott

Jan Michael Vincent

It didn't remain the same breed of dog for long. While the dogfighters, like the bullbaiters before them, never wanted and never bred a dog who was aggressive toward people, the thugs had something else in mind. With no knowledge of genetics or dog breeding, they indiscriminately mated their dogs to larger and nastier dogs of any breed. The result was mixed-breed dogs that the punks still proudly and defiantly called Pit Bulls. They used them to terrorize their enemies, guard drug caches, and slow down the police during drug raids. These dogs, now mixed with Rottweilers, various Shepherds and even mean mongrels, are no more American Pit Bull Terriers than puppies from a Border Collie–Labrador Retriever cross are still Border Collies. But the press, and sometimes the courts, still persist in lumping the mobster's mongrels with registered dogs.

Today, the media still loves its monster. After all, Pit Bulls sell papers and attract TV viewers. A few years ago, for example, there was a *New York Post* story about a man who was attacked and severely bitten on the leg by a dog of another breed. He called the local media, but they didn't find it exciting enough to report. So a few days later, out of curiosity, he falsely told the same story to the same media, but this time he said the dog was a Pit Bull. Three television news stations and four newspapers sent reporters immediately.

The result of the rash of Pit Bull headlines across the nation was that some cities sought to pass laws banning the breed. These were challenged by the ADOA, the major dog registries and dog owners in general, as dog clubs dedicated to all breeds soon realized that if one breed were banned, others could easily follow. In most cases, breed-specific wording was revised and the laws that eventually went into effect were vicious-dog laws that encompassed all dogs equally.

The Pit Bull Today

The real American Pit Bull Terrier, the one registered with the UKC or the ADBA, is the same affectionate, reliable, hard-working, people-loving dog it ever was. A multi-talented companion, the well-trained Pit Bull is suited for a variety of exciting activities. She excels at obedience, agility and weight-pulling competitions, events which showcase intelligence, trainability and strength. In addition, the Pit Bull's pleasant nature makes her an ideal candidate for therapy work with people. Today, because dog shows emphasize balanced structure and fluid movement, and obedience competition emphasizes trainability, the Pit Bull is sometimes an even more attractive companion then she used to be. In addition, the breed still functions as a farm dog in rural America. The Pit Bull began her ranch work on the homesteads of frontier America and is still depended upon for varmint control, rounding up stock and sometimes even stopping and holding an angry steer.

The American Pit Bull Terrier has always been a dog with a strong desire to please her owner. When that owner wanted her to fight, no matter how over-matched the dog was, the Pit Bull fought gamely. And today, when an enlightened owner raises her to be a happy, dependable family companion, that is exactly what she becomes. No dog does it better.

chapter 3

The **World**
According to the
American
Pit Bull Terrier

The American Pit Bull Terrier, whose ancestors were created to compete in the most violent blood sports, became mentally and physically strong. His predecessors survived by strength, intelligence and courage long past the time when survival of the fittest played a role in the propagation of other domestic animals. Therefore, the Pit Bull has remained a functional, capable dog, one who confidently undertakes the roles of watchdog, competitive weight puller, show dog, agility dog, obedience competitor, and children's companion and protector.

Robust, quick and brimming with vigor, today's American Pit Bull Terrier is an intelligent roughneck who wants to please and is ever hopeful of being a lap dog. Supremely confident, he views the world as a giant playhouse created especially for his amusement and is something of a perennial puppy: he enjoys playing tug, catch and other games, well into old age. Good-natured with children, the Pit Bull has the sturdiness not to mind if his tail or toe is accidentally stepped on, and possesses the capacity to play for hours. Some Pit Bulls even seem to sense which children enjoy rough-and-tumble games and which ones are too tiny for such shenanigans. The Pit Bull also enjoys training sessions, and learns quickly as long as his trainer is fair, firm and praises a job well done.

How did a breed that was created to slaughter its own kind become a fine family pet? To find out, we have to visualize a traditional pit fight.

When a dogfighter wanted to match a dog, he or she decided what would be the best fighting weight for that dog and then opened it up to be matched at that weight. The news was conveyed through the underground world of the dogfighting fraternity, and eventually someone else agreed to match their dog at that weight. Forfeit money was posted with a trusted third party, and sometimes a written contract was signed.

After the fight was scheduled, the dogs were put into a "keep." A keep is a regimen of exercise and diet, designed to bring a fighting dog to top strength and endurance and without an extra ounce of weight. During a keep, the handler would utilize roadwork, a treadmill and a swim tank, rubbing the dog thoroughly after his exercise sessions. The keep could last anywhere from six weeks to three months, during which time the handler spent several hours a day preparing the dog.

When the handlers and dogs arrived at the fight, a coin was tossed and the winner of the toss chose whether their dog would be washed first or last. Opponents washed each other's dogs just before a match. This ensured that neither dog had an evil-tasting substance, or even poison, on his coat to deter or kill the rival dog.

After each dog was washed and dried, he was wrapped in a towel and carried to his own corner of the pit. The dog knew why he was there: he wouldn't be matched if he hadn't either fought before or been rolled often enough to understand his owner's game. (In dogfighter jargon, a roll is a short practice fight to see if a young dog has pit potential and to give him experience.)

Because they knew what was coming next, the dogs were usually agitated by the time they were carried to the pit, and their handlers often tried to calm them in order to conserve their energy.

The match began as soon as the referee gave the release order. When the dogs charged viciously at each other, there were three people in the pit with them: two handlers and the referee. Spectators and bettors around the pit sometimes numbered in the hundreds.

Most Pit Bulls fought silently. Using a combination of power and agility, they wrestled each other in an attempt to gain the advantage of their favorite hold. Pit Bull history books about renowned leg fighters or famous ear fighters referred to the dog's favorite place to grip his opponent. Once a fighting dog clamped down his jaws, he usually would not release his grip until he saw the opportunity to get a better one, or until the other dog maneuvered himself free. For this reason, the majority of dogfight wounds were punctures, not rips and slashes. Matches would slow down considerably when both dogs seemed satisfied with their holds. Sometimes neither one moved for several minutes, except to shake his foe.

A DOG'S SENSES

Sight: With their eyes located farther apart than ours, dogs can detect movement at a greater distance than we can, but they can't see as well up close. They can also see better in less light, but can't distinguish many colors.

Sound: Dogs can hear about four times better than we can, and they can hear high-pitched sounds especially well. Their ancestors, the wolves, howled to let other wolves know where they were; our dogs do the same, but they have a wider range of vocalizations, including barks, whimpers, moans and whines.

Smell: A dog's nose is his greatest sensory organ. His sense of smell is so great he can follow a trail that's weeks old, detect odors diluted to one-millionth the concentration we'd need to notice them, even sniff out a person under water!

Taste: Dogs have fewer taste buds than we do, so they're likelier to try anything—and usually do, which is why it's especially important for their owners to monitor their food intake. Dogs are omnivores, which means they eat meat as well as vegetable matter like grasses and weeds.

Touch: Dogs are social animals and love to be petted, groomed and played with.

During a match, the handlers were often right down on the mat beside their dogs, sometimes whispering to them or cheering them on. They were not allowed to touch their dogs unless ordered to do so by the referee. Sometimes dogs became fanged (they caught their own lip with their tooth). When this happened, most referees tried to free the lip themselves, using a pencil to push the lip back up over the tooth. If the referee could not loosen the trapped lip, he or she would order the dogs parted. Then the handlers used breaking sticks (wedge-shaped wooden implements that pried open a dog's mouth) to break the dogs' holds on each other. After the handler of the fanged dog freed his lip, the referee would ask the handlers to face the dogs four feet apart and release them to continue fighting.

When a dog turned his head and shoulders away from his challenger, a turn was called. That meant the handlers had to pick up their dogs and take them back to their respective corners as soon as neither dog had a hold on the other. When each dog was back in his corner, the handler of the turned dog released him. To continue to be a contender, the dog would have to "scratch" (cross the pit and attack the other dog within ten seconds). From then on, the dogs scratched in turn. When a dog failed to scratch, or a handler conceded the match to save the dog's life, the fight ended. A dog who failed to scratch was said to lack gameness and was usually euthanized. A dog who was badly beaten but continued to scratch with gusto was considered game. Such a dog was highly regarded, even if his handler conceded the fight to save his life.

Now that Pit Bulls are not pit fighters, they have more time to spend with their friends.

31

The Personality of a Pit Dog

Contrary to popular hysteria and media hype, the dog-fighting fraternity neither bred nor trained the Pit Bull to be aggressive toward people. Imagine anyone wanting to work with a dangerous dog for hours every day in a keep! And how many handlers would agree to a match if they thought they would have to bathe the other handler's vicious man-biter before the fight? Referees would also be in short supply if unfanging strange dogs during the fury of battle resulted in the loss of fingers. In fact, because they were handled in all sorts of circumstances, fighting dogs had to be friendly, steady and reliable around people. During the era of bullbaiting, when the bull tossed a dog, her owner tried to break her fall by catching her on his own shoulders. As hurt and angry as the dogs were, they didn't misplace their aggression by biting their owner instead of the bull.

Today, a properly bred Pit Bull is so exuberantly happy upon meeting her owner's friends (or even friendly strangers) that new owners sometimes worry that their dog is too sweet and fun-loving to protect their home and family. Never fear: the joyous tail thumper who greets a friendly stranger without hesitation is the same dog who will steadfastly stop an unfriendly stranger. In fact, one of the attributes of the Pit Bull is her ability to tell the difference between friend and foe. This breed doesn't need any formal training to be a forceful, competent and natural guardian.

The protective instinct of the American Pit Bull Terrier usually surfaces when the dog is around ten months old, although this time can vary by three months or so. A Pit Bull with the correct temperament will not threaten to attack a human without a very good reason, but will begin becoming alert to the doorbell or the sight

---

CHARACTERISTICS OF THE AMERICAN PIT BULL TERRIER

Strong resolve to please her owner

Protective instinct—makes her a natural guardian

Enjoys being the center of attention

Highly trainable

Robust and enegetic

of a stranger approaching the house. The young dog doesn't need any encouragement to guard his owners and his home and is best allowed to use his own discretion. There have been numerous cases proving the exceptional ability of the family Pit Bull to sense, and signal to his family, when a person or a situation could be dangerous. Exceptions to letting a Pit Bull guard at will should be made if the dog is overly aggressive, or if he is destined to be used in a specific type of protection work.

From their fighting past Pit Bulls have developed unique temperament traits. One of these is their ability to be selectively aggressive and affectionate, and not to take out their aggression on a human. Necessary in the pit, this trait allowed handlers to safely pick up their dog during a fight.

In civilized circumstances, the trait sometimes shows up when a Pit Bull is out for a walk on a leash and is eyed, menacingly, by another dog. The Pit Bull's immediate reaction might be to face the other dog, ready to take it on. If the Pit Bull is trained, however, and his owner jerks back on the lead to discipline him for a breech of manners, the dog will often lick his owner in apology. A Pit Bull without sufficient training may go back to threatening the other dog after making up with his owner. The breed has the ability to display anger in one direction and love in the other, back and forth, time and again, without ever misdirecting the aggression.

Pit Bulls are excellent at discerning when to show affection and when to show aggression.

The earliest records of the Bull-and-Terrier dogs in England show that many of the top fighting dogs had multiple owners. Today, Pit Bulls are known for being highly adaptable. They can change owners and move to another home with ease, provided their new family gives them attention and love.

Pit Bulls enjoy being the center of attention, are confident enough to adapt to unusual surroundings and have a higher than usual tolerance for pain. These traits place them among the top breeds in canine therapy work. They gleefully show off their obedience training or their favorite tricks at children's hospitals, senior centers and schools for the mentally and physically challenged. Petting sessions often follow the programs, and Pit Bulls excel at giving affection in institutions because they aren't bothered by an occasional bump from a cane or walker. Laying their heads in the laps of the elderly in rockers and children in wheelchairs, they look up lovingly and grunt happily, even when petted or poked a little too hard.

Eternal show-offs, Pit Bulls love exhibiting their talents.

Pit Bulls exude self-confidence, not only at home, but in the park or noisy city street as well. They don't

respect territorial rights as so many other breeds do, but act as if whatever property they happen to be standing on is theirs. While the degree of aggression toward other dogs varies between individuals, Pit Bulls are often so self-assured that they ignore dogs of other breeds rather than pick fights to prove themselves. But this is not always the case. You should be aware that from nine months of age on, your Pit Bull could suddenly develop a desire to test her strength against other dogs. That's one of the reasons why training (see chapter 8) is so important.

Some Pit Bulls of either sex are maternal with baby animals of almost any species, and females have been known to wet-nurse almost anything, from orphaned kittens to Potbellied Pigs. Although most Pit Bulls dislike strange cats, they will live peacefully with the family cat.

Comical Communication

One reason American Pit Bull Terriers are so much fun is that their faces are so expressive. Some of them actually smile. These special canine clowns greet their owners, and sometimes other human friends, with a large toothy grin. They make this amusing mug by raising their upper lip until their muzzle wrinkles and their eyes narrow. When smiling, many Pit Bulls also tap their front feet up and down in a happy dance, demonstrating their delight at the sight of a loved one. While this facial expression is comical and endearing to those who know the breed, it has been known to terrify friendly strangers.

Some breeds are uncomfortable meeting a human's look head on, but not the American Pit Bull Terrier. Not only do they seem to enjoy looking directly into a person's eyes, but they have a charming way of wrinkling their foreheads and cocking their heads, demonstrating that they are giving you their absolute attention.

Even Pit Bulls enjoy relaxing at the beach.

When a Pit Bull believes she has been treated unfairly or slighted, she may turn her back on her owner and refuse to look directly at him or her. This behavior appears to be the dog's way of declaring, "We're not on speaking terms right now." But Pit Bulls are too devoted and fun-loving to hold a grudge for long, so if your dog tries to take you on a guilt trip, let her pout in peace and she will soon be back at your side.

Defective Dogs

American Pit Bull Terriers with temperament problems are rare exceptions, but these exceptions must be mentioned because a dangerous disposition is a menace to your family, your neighbors and the breed itself. Every breed produces occasional problem dogs who never become enjoyable companions, but the Pit Bull is simply too strong and capable to be allowed mental instability. Beware of the extremes: dogs who are either aggressive or extremely timid around people. Pit Bulls who are aggressive toward people are not representative of the breed and are far too dangerous to be pets. Painfully shy dogs are also atypical and may bite out of fear.

Good breeders are careful to choose animals of fine character for breeding stock, but, infrequently, a bad one may still emerge. Even with the best breeding pair, rare problems, such as too little oxygen during birth or a tumor on the brain, can destroy what would have been a delightful disposition.

While bad temperaments due to heredity are rare in ADBA or UKC registered American Pit Bull Terriers, some dogs become unstable because of their environment. Here are the three most common reasons why a perfectly nice puppy might grow up to be mentally defective:

1. Some people delight in owning a dangerous dog. Such people might acquire a friendly little puppy and encourage him to become mean. Eager to please, the dog will grow up to be just as bad as his owner desires.

2. Unfair and overly harsh discipline can reduce an outgoing pup to a cowering bundle of nerves—the first step on the way to biting out of fear. Patience, persistence and praise are essential when working with puppies, and no one should ever train a dog of any age when they are in a bad mood.

3. Neglect probably negates more happy-go-lucky puppy personalities than any other sin of dog ownership. Seldom done on purpose, it just seems to happen when the novelty of having a puppy wears off. Soon the youngster is constantly confined to a crate, tie-out chain, kennel or yard, with no human contact except at feeding time. Lonely, bored and

isolated from his human family, the puppy will be unable to develop his unique character, and could become aloof, shy or cranky.

Personality Traits of Happy Pit Bull Owners

If dogs could choose their owners instead of the other way around, American Pit Bull Terriers would probably look for owners who are blessed with high spirits and the joy of living. This breed some-times bolts around and around the room simply to convey her own delight in life. The Pit Bull still wants to frolic long after her muzzle turns gray, and most con-tented owners enjoy playing with their dogs. In fact, many people consider the breed's perennial puppiness an endearing plus!

Many Pit Bull owners are enthusi-astic, competitive, or both. Since the breed shares its owners' enthusiasm and excels in the showring, obedience competition, weight pulling, agility demonstrations and Schutzhund, many exciting sports are available. Owners who have enthusiasm but don't want to become involved in weekend competitions may find volunteer work with a pet therapy group very fulfilling. Descriptions of these activities appear in chapters 9 and 11.

Your dog will have a happier life if your personality and hers are compatible.

Good owners of American Pit Bull Terriers are able to handle their dogs. The general rule of dog strength is that a dog is approximately as strong as a human three times her weight. That means a 60-pound Pit Bull is as strong as a physically fit 180-pound man.

Does that mean only muscle men should own Pit Bulls? No way! Well-trained American Pit Bull Terriers are often beautifully handled by children. What's im-portant is that the Pit Bull must be trained: successful owners know this and are willing to take on the responsibility and joy of training their dog. If the dog will be handled by a child, the child should understand the basics of training.

Attractive Opposites

Strong and sensitive; rowdy, yet gentle; outgoing, but devoted; easily fired up, but highly trainable; mischievous, yet sensible; energetic and serene; peaceful, but ever alert—these apparent contradictions could all describe the American Pit Bull Terrier. A zest for life, combined with occasional attempts to outwit her owner, endears the breed to many, but could be considered an inconvenience by others. Some people would enjoy a little less dog.

More Information on American Pit Bull Terriers

NATIONAL BREED CLUB

American Dog Breeders Association, Inc. (ADBA)
P.O. Box 1771
Salt Lake City, UT 84110
(801) 936-7513
http://members.aol.com/bstofshw.com

The club can give you information on all aspects of the breed, including the names and addresses of clubs in your area. Inquire about membership.

BOOKS

Coile, D. Caroline. *Pit Bulls for Dummies.* New York: Howell Book House, 2001.

Colby, Louis B., and Diane Jessup. *Colby's Book of the American Pit Bull Terrier.* Neptune, New Jersey: TFH Publications, 1997.

Fraser, Jacqueline. *The Ultimate Pit Bull Terrier.* New York: Howell Book House, 1995.

Stahlkuppe, Joe. *The American Pit Bull Terrier Handbook.* New York: Barrons Educational Series, 2000.

MAGAZINES

The American Pit Bull Terrier Gazette
American Dog Breeders Association, Inc. (ADBA)
P.O. Box 1771
Salt Lake City, UT 84110
(801) 936-7513
http://members.aol.com/bstofshw/wlcm.html

Pit Bull Reporter Magazine
282 Dick Finch Road
Romance, AR 72136
pitbulls@pitbulls.com, or www.pitbulls.com

WEB SITES

The United Kennel Club (UKC)
www.ukcdogs.com
The United Kennel Club was the first breed organization to recognize the American Pit Bull Terrier. The UKC's Web site, www.ukcdogs.com, offers comprehensive information on the American Pit Bull Terrier. The UKC also publishes the magazine *Bloodlines*, which contains information and event listings related to Pit Bulls. To order, call (616) 343-9020 or write *Bloodlines*, 100 East Kilgore Road, Kalamazoo, MI 49002-5584.

The American Pit Bull Terrier (APBT)
www.apbt.com
This site provides comprehensive information on the American Pit Bull Terrier. Visitors can surf to find out about rescue organizations, view photographs of Pit Bull charmers and their people, scrutinize kennels, purchase American Pit Bull Terrier–related gift items or learn how to fight breed-specific legislation.

Pit Bull Reporter Magazine, online edition
www.pitbulls.com
This energetic site is the electronic version of the *Pit Bull Reporter Magazine.* Come visit for information on all things pro Pit Bull. Readers are urged to respond to topics that they find interesting or controversial. The paper edition is published every two months. You can also e-mail directly to pitbulls@pitbulls.com.

Living
with an

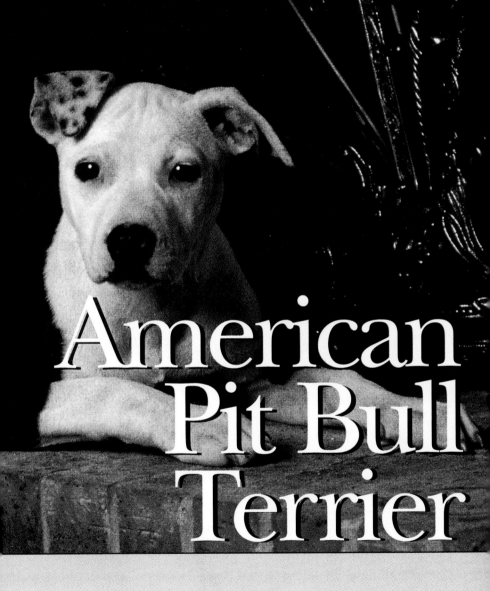

part two

American Pit Bull Terrier

chapter 4

Bringing your
American
Pit Bull Terrier
Home

A little advance planning will help you enjoy your new dog and will keep him happy and healthy. Before bringing "Beau" home, you will want to have nutritious puppy food in the cupboard and the address and phone number of a trusted veterinarian.

Exercise: Leading an active life will make Beau live longer, look healthier and behave better. Brisk walks are good for both of you. If you don't want to walk every day, teach Beau to play ball or frisbee and you can exercise him while sitting or standing, or give him a securely fenced play area with a couple of dog toys and an old car tire, and he will exercise himself. Many Pit Bulls love to play with tires and get sufficient exercise by wrestling with them.

Sleepy Time: Young puppies tire easily and should be allowed to sleep until they wake up on their own. Even the healthiest, happiest pups become limp as dishrags when it's snooze time, and when puppies are young, naps are sudden, frequent and often short. As puppies grow older, they sleep less often but stay asleep for a longer time.

Puppyproofing Your Home

Until Beau is housebroken and has stopped teething, confine him to one easily cleaned room of your home when no one is home to supervise him. The kitchen or bathroom is ideal; basements and garages are too isolated to teach a puppy how to be part of the family. A wire mesh baby gate (rather than easily chewed plastic or wood) often works better than a door when confining a young puppy to a room.

To make the room (and the rest of your home) safe when Beau is unsupervised, put all cleaning agents, antifreeze, pesticides, drugs, and other household, garage or garden chemicals out of his reach. If it isn't possible to eliminate electrical wires that Beau can reach, coat them with Bitter Apple, a safe, bad-tasting substance created to prevent chewing. If you have houseplants, identify them and look them up to make sure they are not poisonous (many common houseplants are). All plants should be placed out of Beau's reach because no puppy is able to resist playing with a plant; extra precautions are necessary with poisonous plants. If you like your nontoxic plants placed where they are but want Beau to learn to leave them alone, spray them with Bitter Apple leaf protector.

Expect an unsupervised puppy to teethe on whatever is reachable. It's important to close cupboard doors because puppies have been known to chomp on anything from raw potatoes to fountain pens and brillo pads. But don't worry. Securing closet and cupboard doors, or flipping the shower curtain up over the rod, aren't so hard to remember once you have your precious puppy.

**PUPPY
ESSENTIALS**

Your new
puppy will
need:

food bowl

water bowl

collar

leash

I. D. tag

bed

crate

toys

grooming
supplies

43

The Great Crate

Dogs are descended from denning animals that spent a great deal of their time in the relative security of their lair. That's why it will take only a brief period of adjustment before Beau feels comfortable and protected in a dog crate. Rather than being cruel, as some new dog owners imagine, dog crates have saved dogs' lives and owners' tempers.

Safeguard your puppy against the perils that could await him in a new home.

Buy baby Beau a crate that is large enough for a grown American Pit Bull Terrier to stand up and turn around in comfortably. The crate will be a tremendous help with housebreaking, because Beau will soon learn not to soil his bed (see chapter 8 for details). It can also serve as a safe playpen, so Beau can't damage furniture or swallow something dangerous when you are away or asleep. The crate should be placed in Beau's puppyproofed room, right up front near the baby gate. Visualize Beau's puppyproofed room as the nursery, and the crate as a combination crib, playpen and car seat, and you'll easily figure out how to use it for your convenience.

If it's impossible to give Beau his own puppyproofed room, you can still enjoy the benefits of a crate. In fact, without the confined area of a room for your puppy, a crate becomes almost essential. Coming home to a safely crated puppy is much nicer, for both of you, than coming home to a messy rug and teeth marks on the furniture.

Beau's crate should be snug, soft and comfortable inside. The bedding should be easy to change and not dangerous if chewed or swallowed. For example, several thicknesses of newspaper (black and white, not color) make good indoor bedding. Every time you put Beau in his crate, toss a favorite toy or a special treat in the crate ahead of him. Say "crate" and, as gently as possible, put Beau in and shut the door. Beau may cry the first few times he is introduced to his crate, but if you walk away and don't take him out of the crate until he settles down, he'll soon become accustomed to it.

Basic Supplies

Safe Toys: Toys are not an extra but a necessity. Beau needs something safe on which to gnaw while he is teething, and should have toys available all the time. Chewing is good for dogs because it helps remove plaque from their teeth and promotes healthy gums. Beau will still enjoy chewing when he grows up, but he won't be driven to mouth everything in sight the way

Even if you let your puppies play outside they will appreciate toys.

teething puppies do. Rawhide chew toys are a traditional favorite, but there have been rare accidents when a torn chunk from a rawhide toy got caught in a dog's throat and choked him. So give Beau rawhide only when you are home and in the same room with him, and don't choose rawhide for his crate toy.

Squeaky toys (of lightweight rubber or plastic) are popular with pups, but they are only safe when you are either watching or joining in the play. These toys are easily torn apart by Pit Bull puppies and swallowed, dangerous squeaker mechanism and all. Keep Beau's squeaky toy out of his reach and bring it out every few days for some special minutes of fun.

Chew toys made of hard nylon are safe in Beau's mouth even when you aren't home. Puppies prefer the softer, equally safe, gummy-type nylon chews. Solid, hard rubber toys are also safe and fun, but eventually

Beau may be able to mangle even those labeled "indestructible." When you see that he is gouging pieces out of his rubber toys, do not leave him alone with them.

Braided rope toys are fun for games of tug, and good for helping to keep Beau's teeth tartar free. If Beau starts unraveling his rope, don't let him alone with it, as swallowing the string could cause intestinal problems. For the ultimate puppy treat, buy a sterilized bone toy and stuff it with cheese. This crate toy will keep Beau occupied for a long time.

Practical Dog Dishes: These are easy to clean and difficult to tip over, and Beau should have one for food and another for water. The food dish should be washed after each use, and the water dish should be refilled with fresh water frequently and washed thoroughly once a day. When selecting dishes, remember that as Beau grows, so will the size of his meals.

Grooming Gizmos: Unlike hairy breeds, Pit Bulls have easy-to-care-for coats. All you need to keep Beau beautiful is a brush with short, soft to medium bristles, a heavy-duty toenail clipper, a good quality pH-balanced dog shampoo (sometimes you may need insecticide shampoo or dip) and a soft toothbrush. The rest of what you need for Beau's bathing and grooming needs is probably already in your medicine chest (see chapter 6 for more information).

First Collar and Leash: Wait until you bring Beau home to buy a collar, so you can get one that will fit his neck perfectly. The collar should apply no pressure to his neck, but it shouldn't be loose enough to slip over

HOUSEHOLD DANGERS

Curious puppies and inquisitive dogs get into trouble not because they are bad, but simply because they want to investigate the world around them. It's our job to protect our dogs from harmful substances, like the following:

IN THE HOUSE

cleaners, especially pine oil

perfumes, colognes, aftershaves

medications, vitamins

office and craft supplies

electric cords

chicken or turkey bones

chocolate

some house and garden plants, like ivy, oleander and poinsettia

IN THE GARAGE

antifreeze

garden supplies, like snail and slug bait, pesticides, fertilizers, mouse and rat poisons his head. It should be flat, made of nylon webbing or leather, with a buckle and ring for attaching the leash. Check the fit of Beau's collar weekly. Puppies grow fast, and collars must be replaced immediately when they become too small.

Beau's leash should be five to six feet long and made of leather, nylon webbing or some other strong, flexible fabric. Neither the collar nor the leash should be made of chain. You may want a chain training collar as a teaching aid when Beau is older, but he should wear it only for training, not as his regular collar.

Poop Scoop: Available in pet supply stores, poop scoops are convenient for cleaning up your yard. It's also important to clean up after Beau when you take him for walks, and in many places, it's the law.

Young puppies need ways to release their energy.

Housing Your American Pit Bull Terrier

No dog should be allowed to run loose, but safe confinement is exceptionally important for a Pit Bull. Out and about without human guidance, your Pit Bull may get into trouble with another dog. You should have a strong sense of responsibility to your breed and your neighbors, and buy or build whatever it takes to keep your dog on your property, and sometimes it may take a lot! Pit Bulls can dig like badgers, and a few of them can clear seven-foot fences from a standstill.

The closer you and your dog live together, the closer your bond becomes. House dogs, provided they get sufficient exercise, are the luckiest dogs of all. Dogs are

social animals and suffer loneliness and boredom when confined to quarters away from human contact.

Where a house dog sleeps depends on you. Allowed free choice, Beau will probably end up in bed with you or one of your children. If such accommodations don't suit you, teach him that beds are off limits. Suitable sleeping arrangements might be a soft pad beside your bed, a doggie bed in your daughter's room, a crate in the kitchen, or a throw rug near the back door.

The Outdoor Dog

If you keep your puppy confined in a safe, clean area he will thrive.

If your Pit Bull will be an outside dog, or will spend part of the day outdoors, it's vital that she have adequate shelter from heat, rain, and cold, and that she be securely confined to your property. The following are several possibilities for safe, outdoor confinement.

The Fenced Yard: A high, well-installed chain-link fence is sufficient for most (but not all) Pit Bulls. Keep a careful eye on the condition of your fence, especially around the bottom where Beau may try to dig his way out; and watch to see if Beau develops exceptional jumping ability. If you already have a chain-link or other securely fenced yard, perhaps all Beau needs is a cozy doghouse.

The Dog Run: A high chain-link kennel run, with six inches of fence buried underground and anchored in cement, a wire roof and a doghouse at one end, should keep Beau where he belongs even if he grows into an Olympic-quality jumper. Shade screen over the wire roof and down one or two sides of the run will help cool the area. Patio blocks, or cement finished to a rough surface, make good, easily cleaned flooring for the pen.

Plan before you build. It's often possible to save money by using one wall of your house or garage as one side of the pen.

Chained: Chances are that more Pit Bulls have been raised on chains than any other way, but this method of confinement should never be used as a substitute for safe fencing. If Beau must be chained because he is an escape artist, chain him in a shady area inside your fenced-in yard. Make sure the chain, the swivel, the collar and all the connections are extremely sturdy and in good working order.

The Doghouse: Many pet supply stores have excellent doghouses for sale, or you can make one yourself. There are only a few requirements to building a good doghouse.

The floor of the doghouse should be raised off the ground two or three inches to protect it from rain, snow, dampness and morning dew. A removable roof, or one on hinges, will make it easier to clean the inside. The door should be to one side of the house and partitioned off, with the sleeping space on the other side away from the drafty door.

To conserve body heat, the sleeping space should be cozy—just the right size for Beau to curl up comfortably.

Like babies, puppies will take frequent naps.

The very best bedding is cedar chips. They smell wonderful, stay clean and dry for a long time and help Beau keep cool in summer and warm in winter. If you can't find cedar bedding, wood shavings are a dependable second choice. Make the bedding deep, especially in winter.

The Freedom Fantasy

Some dog owners think they are doing an injustice to their dog unless they let him experience freedom. In fact, seven million loose dogs die every year due to accidents. Besides being killed by cars, loose dogs may eat poisonous substances, get picked up by animal control officers and can be a menace to livestock, cats, the neighbor's flower bed and other dogs. Seven million dead dogs is a lot, and putting yours in a position to become a statistic isn't doing him a favor. Beau is a domestic animal. Instead of freedom, give him what he really wants—your companionship.

chapter 5

Feeding
your
American
Pit Bull Terrier

Good nutrition is essential to prevent dietary deficiency diseases. It also helps ward off infections and reduces your Pit Bull's susceptibility to diseases.

What Does What in Your Dog's Food

All dogs require food containing the proper proportions of carbohydrates, proteins, fats, vitamins and minerals.

Carbohydrates aid digestion and elimination, and provide energy and the proper assimilation of fats.

51

Excess carbohydrates are stored in the body for future use.

Protein is not stored, so your Pit Bull must receive it every day of her life. It is used for bone growth, tissue healing and the daily replacement of body tissues burned up by normal activity.

Always make sure to clean your dog's bowl after she is done eating to keep it clear of bacteria and bugs.

Fat is necessary as an energy source and adds shine to your dog's coat and suppleness to her skin. But excess fat is stored under the skin and can result in an overweight dog. The fat balance is important. Too much fat leads to the same obesity problems that humans sometimes suffer from, while too little will not provide your Pit Bull with protection from changes of temperature, and can result in a dog who is overly sensitive to cold.

Vitamin A is necessary for a healthy, shiny coat because it is used by your dog's body for fat absorption. It is also essential for normal growth rate, reproduction and good eyesight. The **B vitamins** protect the nervous system and are also necessary for normal coat, skin, appetite, growth and eyes. Dogs synthesize **Vitamin C** in their own livers, so it is not often mentioned in an analysis of commercial dog food or vitamin preparations. Some breeders add it anyway, believing that it aids healing in the event of injury, helps prevent hip dysplasia and fights bacterial infections. Healthy bones, teeth and muscle tone are all dependent upon **Vitamin D,** but the vitamin must be taken in the correct ratio with calcium and phosphorus. **Vitamin E** is associated with the proper functioning of the muscles and the internal and reproductive organs. Most dogs are able to synthesize **Vitamin K** in their digestive tract; it is essential to the normal clotting of blood, so if your dog seems to bleed too much and too long from a minor cut, mention it to your veterinarian. It could indicate a lack of Vitamin K.

Calcium and **Phosphorus** must be not only present but in the correct ratio, to provide puppies with protection from rickets, bowed legs and other bone deformities. These elements also aid muscle development and maintenance, as well as lactation in nursing bitches.

Your Pit Bull needs **Potassium** for normal growth, healthy nerves and muscles; **Sodium** and **Chlorine** to maintain appetite and allow her to enjoy a normal activity level; **Magnesium** to prevent convulsions and problems with the nervous system; **Iron** for the healthy blood that prevents fatigue from anemia; and **Iodine** to prevent goiter.

Copper is necessary for growing and maintaining strong bones and, like iron, it helps prevent anemia. **Cobalt** aids normal growth and keeps the reproductive tract healthy. **Manganese** also aids growth and is utilized in reproduction. **Zinc** is involved in normal growth and also promotes healthy skin.

Using Commercial Dog Food

Most commercially prepared dog foods are balanced to provide your dog with optimal nutrition and are far healthier than anything you could create at home for twice the price. The proper balance of vitamins and minerals, fats and proteins, is too complicated and too

HOW MANY MEALS A DAY?

Individual dogs vary in how much they should eat to maintain a desired body weight—not too fat, but not too thin. Puppies need several meals a day, while older dogs may need only one. Determine how much food keeps your adult dog looking and feeling her best. Then decide how many meals you want to feed with that amount. Like us, most dogs love to eat, and offering two meals a day is more enjoyable for them. If you're worried about overfeeding, make sure you measure correctly and abstain from adding tidbits to the meals.

Whether you feed one or two meals, only leave your dog's food out for the amount of time it takes her to eat it—10 minutes, for example. Freefeeding (when food is available any time) and leisurely meals encourage picky eating. Don't worry if your dog doesn't finish all her dinner in the allotted time. She'll learn she should.

important to guess at, and is better left to the test kitchens of the major dog food companies. Another danger is our human tendency to think that if some of a substance is good for bones or appetite or nerves, than a lot will probably be better. This assumption is definitely not true, and in some cases, larger doses are actually toxic.

Commercial dog foods fall into three major categories: canned, dry and semimoist. When planning to use only canned food, it is important to read the label carefully. Some canned foods provide total nutrition, but others are formulated to be mixed with dry food. If the canned food is meant to be used alone, it will say some-

A good quality dog food should fulfill all of your dog's nutritional needs.

thing like "100 percent complete" or "complete dinner" on the label. Some canned dinners are available either "chopped" or "chunky." The nutritional values are equal, but most puppies find it easier to eat the chopped variety, while adult Pit Bulls often prefer their food "chunky."

Dry dog foods come in a variety of shapes and sizes. Some types are in meal form, with the ingredients simply mixed together. Biscuit food may be made up of whole biscuits or crumbled biscuits. It is formed by adding flour to the dry ingredients and baking the mixture. Some dog foods are pelleted, by which meal-type food is pressed into pellet form. Read the labels on the dry food you buy, because some are meant to be used dry, others form gravy when moistened and are meant to be used slightly wet, and some may be fed to your dog dry or moistened. Many Pit Bulls have been fed dry food exclusively and lived healthy, active lives. Another popular and wholesome feed is a two-thirds dry and one-third canned food mixture.

While convenient and less expensive than the better quality canned foods, semimoist food usually is high in salt, sugar and preservatives. Although it's tempting because of its simplicity, you can get the same ease of feeding by packing portions of high-quality dry food in self-sealing baggies. Good dry formulas are better for your dog and even help to clean her teeth.

Nutrition throughout Your Dog's Life

Bargain dog food is seldom a bargain. Even though the nutritional information on the package says it has the same amount of protein as the better-known brands, what's important is the amount of usable (digestible) protein. For example, shoe leather is protein, but it has no nutritional value at all. There is a fine selection of dog foods available for all stages of your dog's life. Choose a reputable brand of puppy food, one that has been on the market for many years, then feed "Maria" according to label directions, and she should be well-nourished. If you change brands from her breeder's brand, mix the new brand with the old, increasing the amount of the new brand gradually until the changeover is complete. Make the change in the same gradual way when Maria reaches a year old and is ready for adult dog food.

While Maria is growing, remember to gradually increase the size of her meals as she gets bigger. At seven

HOW TO READ THE DOG FOOD LABEL

With so many choices on the market, how can you be sure you are feeding the right food for your dog? The information is all there on the label—if you know what you're looking for.

Look for the nutritional claim right up top. Is the food "100% nutritionally complete"? If so, it's for nearly all life stages; "growth and maintenance," on the other hand, is for early development; puppy foods are marked as such, as are foods for senior dogs.

Ingredients are listed in descending order by weight. The first three or four ingredients will tell you the bulk of what the food contains. Look for the highest-quality ingredients, like meats and grains, to be among them.

The Guaranteed Analysis tells you what levels of protein, fat, fiber and moisture are in the food, in that order. While these numbers are meaningful, they won't tell you much about the quality of the food. Nutritional value is in the dry matter, not the moisture content.

In many ways, seeing is believing. If your dog has bright eyes, a shiny coat, a good appetite and a good energy level, chances are his diet's fine. Your dog's breeder and your veterinarian are good sources of advice if you're still confused.

weeks old, she will need to eat three meals a day. By the time she is five months old, she will probably need about twice what she ate when she was three months old, but she doesn't have to eat as often. By then, two meals a day are sufficient. As an adult (over twelve months old), Maria will probably eat slightly less than she did as a growing puppy and will only need to eat once a day. Look at her to tell whether or not her food keeps her in top condition. Maria's coat should shine, her eyes should be bright and she should have good, solid flesh. Whatever you do, don't allow her to become fat. Roly-poly puppies may look cute, but many serious health problems in dogs have been traced directly to obesity.

During adolescence (five to eleven months or more of age), Maria may appear rangy and gangly, but as long as she has boundless energy and a gleaming coat, her nutritional requirements are probably being met. Poor nutrition almost always shows up first in the quality of the coat. If Maria's coat is dry or dull, consider it an early warning signal that something is wrong. Have your veterinarian examine Maria, because it's possible that the quality and quantity of her food are fine but that she might need to be wormed or treated for a condition unrelated to nutrition. If her nutritional needs are not being met, your veterinarian may recommend that you change brands of dog food. This must be done gradually, and it will be several weeks before you will see a difference.

TYPES OF FOODS/TREATS

There are three types of commercially available dog food—dry, canned and semimoist—and a huge assortment of treats (lucky dogs!) to feed your dog. Which should you choose?

Dry and canned foods contain similar ingredients. The primary difference between them is their moisture content. The moisture is not just water. It's blood and broth, too, the very things that dogs adore. So while canned food is more palatable, dry food is more economical, convenient and effective in controlling tartar buildup. Most owners feed a 25% canned/75% dry diet to give their dogs the benefit of both. Just be sure your dog is getting the nutrition he needs (you and your veterinarian can determine this).

Semimoist food have the flavor dogs love and the convenience owners want. However, they tend to contain excessive amounts of artificial colors and preservatives.

Dog treats come in every size, shape and flavor imaginable, from organic cookies shaped like postmen to beefy chew sticks. Dogs seem to love them all, so enjoy the variety. Just be sure not to overindulge your dog. Factor treats into her regular meal sizes.

Some owners like to supplement their dog's diet with vitamins. Over-supplementation is dangerous and has been linked to a variety of ills, including hip dysplasia, so if you want Maria to take vitamins, give them according to your veterinarian's directions.

Many adult dogs retain their proper weight consistently when given a little extra food during the winter and a little less during the heat of summer. Maria may show less interest in her food during the warm months and turn into a "chowhound" by November.

There is no reason to change dog foods after you find a high-quality, well-respected one that Maria enjoys, provided she feels well and looks good after six months of eating it. Dog foods have eye appeal to attract you, not your dog. Dogs won't get bored with the same food every day as people would, and don't need to discover new shapes, colors and sizes in their bowls at frequent intervals. As long as you are feeding a recognized, high-quality food and your dog is thriving, it is unlikely that any change would be for the better.

When Maria grows old, she may show less interest in her food for a number of reasons. One of them is sore teeth. If dental problems are causing Maria pain, your veterinarian can give you advice on how to make feeding time a pleasure again. If age is dulling Maria's senses, warming her food will give it a more appetizing aroma. Also, offering much smaller amounts of food several times a day, instead of one big dinner, sometimes entices an old dog to eat.

Older dogs do better when fed a dog food with a lower percentage of protein than they ate during their prime years. Change should be made gradually, and is usually easiest on the dog when you stick to the brand that proved successful but go to a formula lower in protein. Most brand-name dog foods come in several varieties, and you can easily find a variety with less protein by reading the nutrition information on the back of the bag. Some brands even make a special formula for older dogs.

There are special times in a dog's life when supplementation may be advisable. Females who have been bred or are lactating may need a little extra food, especially if their appetites are suffering. Show dogs may be stressed from constantly traveling and competing. If you think your American Pit Bull Terrier might benefit from supplements, check with your veterinarian. He or she may suggest the addition of cottage cheese, hardboiled (never raw) eggs, raw beef liver or a little fat to your dog's diet, or may put the dog on a prepared vitamin-mineral powder or tablet.

Cleaning Chores

Maria's food and water dishes must be kept clean. Wash them daily to prevent the growth of disease-producing bacteria and other dangerous microorganisms. Also, her play area should be frequently cleaned with a poop scoop, which will help control worms and biting insects.

Easily Avoided Errors

1. *Don't feed your Pit Bull chocolate or any highly spiced, greasy or salty foods.* Chocolate is deadly to some dogs, and spicy sauces and junk food lead to stomach upsets.

2. *Don't believe ads that encourage you to vary your dog's diet.* Dogs do best when they are fed the same brand of food daily at a regular hour. If you must add something to your Pit Bull's food dish, mix a few tablespoons of a high-quality canned dog food with his dry dinner.

3. *Don't fill your puppy up with table scraps.* Puppies can't hold much food at a time, and no matter how nutritious your dinner is for humans, chances are your puppy's food is better for her. Also, dogs who eat table scraps often lose their taste for dog food completely. It's especially important not to feed your dog directly from the table. Dogs fed during dinner become accomplished beggars and are soon a major nuisance at mealtimes.

4. *Don't give your Pit Bull any bones other than cooked knuckle bones.* Chicken, turkey, or pork chop bones, for example, can shatter and slice open the dog's intestines with their sharp points.

5. *Don't leave your Pit Bull's food dish down for longer than 10 minutes.* If the dog hasn't finished her food by then, remove it until the next feeding. That helps your dog learn to eat when and what she is fed.

6. *Don't forget to take along food and water from home when taking your dog on a long outing or on vacation.* In an unfamiliar area, it may be difficult to find the same food to which your dog is accustomed, and an abrupt change of diet frequently gives dogs enough stomach trouble to spoil a vacation. It's also a good idea to take along water from home. Although strange water doesn't sicken dogs as easily as strange food does, the chemicals added in various locales may give the water an unfamiliar odor. Some dogs seem to distrust such water and either refuse it entirely or do not drink enough of it. If you didn't bring water from home and your dog refuses to drink, buy enough bottled water for one day. At the same time, put a couple quarts of the local water in a wide-mouth container and allow it to sit for 24 hours before giving it to your dog. Usually that allows the odor to dissipate enough so that your dog will drink it.

TO SUPPLEMENT OR NOT TO SUPPLEMENT?

If you're feeding your dog a diet that's correct for her developmental stage and she's alert, healthy-looking and neither over- nor underweight, you don't need to add supplements. These include table scraps as well as vitamins and minerals. In fact, a growing puppy is in danger of developing musculoskeletal disorders by oversupplementation. If you have any concerns about the nutritional quality of the food you're feeding, discuss them with your veterinarian.

Following these feeding guides will help your American Pit Bull Terrier stay as happy and healthy as possible.

chapter 6

Grooming
your
American
Pit Bull Terrier

Grooming your American Pit Bull Terrier will soon become a pleasant, relaxing part of your daily routine. It takes less than five minutes a day to keep Maria clean and shiny, but you will accomplish much more than that. Grooming feels good to you and your dog and will strengthen the bond between you. It will also save you money. Inspecting Maria for external parasites, minor injuries and early signs of skin disease while grooming helps you find and solve small problems before they become big, expensive ones.

There are few jobs more difficult than trimming the nails of a mature, 50-pound Pit Bull who is not accustomed to having her feet touched. But if you condition Maria from puppyhood to accept grooming as a regular part of life, she will soon learn that being handled and brushed is both pleasant and serious: pleasant because it feels good, serious because she is expected to behave. If Maria becomes fidgety about being handled on any part of her body, tell her "NO" sharply and firmly. By the time she is half grown, she should be steady and cooperative when you groom her.

Brushing

Daily brushing will make Maria sparkle because brushing removes dander, dirt and dead hair, while stimulating the secretion of natural oils that keep her coat sleek and shiny. Two types of brushes will be effective on Maria. The first (and the one you will use most often), can be a hand-held brush with medium-soft bristles or a glove type of brush, which usually has horsehair bristles. Brush Maria's coat gently but firmly in the direction of growth. When no more loose hair or dander comes out and her coat gleams, you have brushed enough. To groom Maria's face, use a damp cloth instead of a brush.

Your second brush should be a rubber curry brush of about palm size, useful after Maria has a romp in the mud. When you can actually see the dirt on her coat, use the curry before using your regular brush. Let the mud dry before you curry, and then curry by moving the rubber brush in small circles all over the upper part of her body. Skip her legs, feet, belly and face (and the genitals on a male), as the curry is too rough for those areas. Your regular brush will easily remove mud from Maria's legs and feet, and a damp cloth will clean her nearly bald belly and her face (and a male's genital area). Maria may just love the curry and lean right into it to show her pleasure. Currying is good for her, and it's okay to begin every grooming session with the curry if you want to (whether you need to or not). Just be sure to finish the job with your regular bristle brush.

Inspect Maria while brushing her. Look for open wounds that need washing and treatment, signs of skin disease, external parasites, and bumps, warts, splinters or anything else that could signal the start of

GROOMING TOOLS

pin brush

slicker brush

flea comb

towel

matt rake

grooming glove

scissors

nail clippers

tooth-cleaning equipment

shampoo

conditioner

clippers

a problem. Remember that ticks sometimes hide between the toes, in the ears, or in the thickest part of your Pit Bull's coat (usually the neck and rump area). Separate Maria's hair by roughing it against the grain to look for fleas. Even if you do not see any fleas, tiny dark specks are evidence that your dog is being used as a bed and breakfast. Ask your veterinarian to recommend preparations to rid Maria (and your home) of such parasites, and use the insecticide formulas exactly as advised on their labels.

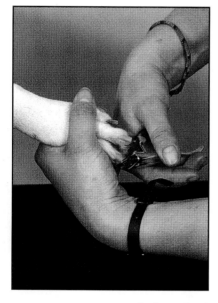

Pick a clean, well-lit area in which to trim your dog's nails.

Teeth and Toenails

To check Maria's teeth for tartar, hold her head firmly and lift her lips upward. A soft toothbrush or damp washcloth dipped in baking soda usually removes discolorations on the teeth. If the stains are not easily removed, ask your veterinarian if Maria's teeth need a professional cleaning. Hard dog biscuits and nylon chew toys will help keep a young dog's teeth white, but are not enough to do the whole job.

Maria's toenails are too long if they make clicking noises on the floor when she walks or touch the ground when she is standing still. Dogs with very long nails tend to walk on the back of their feet, leading to splayed toes and an unattractive gait. Not only is this uncomfortable for the dog, but there is an additional danger. If untrimmed, toenails and dewclaws eventually curl under the foot, circling back to puncture the pads. This problem doesn't occur in wolves, coyotes or even stray dogs, because in their quest for food, they cover enough ground to wear their toenails down to a practical length.

To clip Maria's nails, lift her foot up and forward. Hold it securely in one hand, allowing your dominant hand to do the trimming. If Maria has white nails, your job is easier than if her nails are dark. There is a blood vessel called the quick in the bottom stem of the nail, which is clearly seen through white nails. Trim the nail just outside the quick. You will not be able to see the quick in dark nails, so make the cut just outside the hooklike projection on the underside of the nail.

When you cut the nail properly, Maria will feel nothing more than slight pressure, the same as you feel when cutting your own toenails. If you accidentally cut the quick, Maria's nail will hurt and bleed. Stop the bleeding with a styptic pencil made for human use, or use the styptic powder sold at pet supply stores. Pressing the bleeding nail into a soft bar of soap for a minute or so will also stop the bleeding. Try to work under good lighting so you can cut Maria's nails without a mishap. She will forgive a cut quick if it is a rare occurrence; but if you are clumsy too often, she may begin to resist work on her feet.

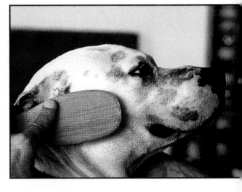

Brushing can actually be soothing and enjoyable for your Pit Bull.

Bathing

Since brushing cleans the coat and reduces body odors, Maria will rarely need a bath if she gets three to five minutes of brushing daily. Bathe her only when necessary, because shampooing dries the coat by washing away natural oils.

Equipment for a bath includes: old clothes (when Maria shakes, you'll be as wet as she is); a tub, preferably with a drain so Maria won't be standing in soapy water; a rubber mat for traction in the tub; a spray-nozzle hose attachment or a pail for dipping water; pH-balanced dog shampoo or insecticide shampoo (and a flea-and-tick dip if necessary); cotton balls; a washcloth; mineral oil; and a large towel or two. Coat conditioner applied after the shampoo is optional.

Before bathing Maria, allow her to exercise outside for a few minutes. That way she won't have to dash outdoors to relieve herself (and probably roll in the loose garden dirt) immediately following her bath.

63

Maria's bath water should be warm but not hot. Begin by placing a cotton ball inside each of her ears, to keep the water out. Next, spray or pour water over Maria's whole body with the exception of her face and head. Put a small amount of shampoo on her back and massage the lather well into her coat. Then add more

Placing your dog on a table will make grooming him easier for you.

shampoo as needed to clean her legs, neck, tail and underbelly. If you accidentally get soap in Maria's eyes, put a few drops of mineral oil in the inner corner of each eye to relieve the sting. Use the hose or pail to thoroughly rinse off the lather. Do not rush this step. Shampoo left to dry in the coat makes it dull and can cause intense itching. If you are using insecticide shampoo or dip, follow the label's directions carefully.

Finish by wiping Maria's face and head with a warm, well-wrung washcloth. Remove the cotton from her ears and wipe them out with a dry cotton ball dipped in a bit of mineral oil. Then wrap Maria in a towel, lift her from the tub, and towel-dry her well, especially her chest and underbelly.

To Crop or Not to Crop

"Ears: Cropped or uncropped (not important)." UKC Breed Standard for the American Pit Bull Terrier

Ear cropping in the bull and terrier breeds had its origins in blood sports. Because ripped ears can bleed profusely, some dogfighters would cut the ears off their dogs so their opponents couldn't get an ear hold. Others left the ears natural, preferring the possibility of a torn ear over a leg, chest or throat hold. Today, ear cropping (sometimes called ear trimming) has no purpose but style, and cropped ears are shaped in an attractive prick-eared fashion.

Most Pit Bull breeders sell their puppies with natural (uncropped) ears, so shortly after you bring Maria home you will have to decide whether you want to have her ears cropped or not. In some countries, this decision does not have to be made. England, for example, outlawed cropping years ago, and Boxers, Schnauzers, Doberman Pinschers, Great Danes and other breeds that are almost always cropped in the United States, retain natural ears there. Someday, ear cropping may also be outlawed in the United States, but right now you still have a choice.

The best way to decide if you want to have Maria's ears cropped is to look at several cropped or uncropped mature Pit Bulls and decide which style appeals to you. Many people feel that cropped dogs have a more alert appearance, while uncropped dogs have a softer expression and are more communicative with their ears.

Some veterinarians who have cropped other breeds may not

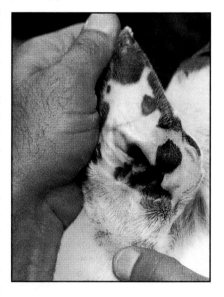

Whether or not you decide to crop your Pit Bull's ears, you should always keep them clean.

have cropped an American Pit Bull Terrier. Consequently, you might make an appointment to have Maria cropped, only to have your veterinarian ask you to describe the proper style for the breed. If this happens, show your veterinarian the following section of this book. It was written by a veterinarian with much experience cropping American Pit Bull Terriers. There are several style variations, but the one described here is easy for a veterinarian who is inexperienced with Pit Bulls to perform successfully. In fact, hundreds of dogs with successful show careers have sported this style.

Cropping the American Pit Bull Terrier
by Bonnie Wilcox, D.V.M.

The correct American Pit Bull Terrier ear crop accentuates the massive head and muscular appearance of the breed. Since the cropped ear is relatively short, there is seldom any difficulty in getting the ear to stand after surgery. Because of the limited need for aftercare, the age for cropping is not as critical as for breeds in which the ear style is much longer. Pit Bull puppies can be cropped at seven to eight weeks; however, waiting until twelve to fourteen weeks presents few problems.

Ear length is determined by laying the ear forward parallel to the eye WITHOUT PULLING OR STRETCHING. The cut is begun just short of where the medial edge of the ear meets the lateral canthus of the eye. Proportionately, it is a bit shorter than a Miniature Schnauzer cut. The shape is distinctive to the American Pit Bull Terrier. There is no graceful curve to the ear as in the Boxer or Dobe. In fact, the ear edge is actually slightly convex from ear tip to base. The base is trimmed back cleanly to form a smooth, flat surface that blends into the cheek and neck.

A well-groomed Pit Bull sitting proud!

A correctly cut ear on a pup looks just slightly longer than the ideal preferred ear. As the dog grows, the ears will become proportional to the head.

Ears that droop outward or hang after stitch removal can be trained to stand by rolling and taping the base. A week or two in tape is usually all that is required. Most American Pit Bull Terrier ears stand without any taping. Ear cartilage forming a crease at the head line can cause problem ears in some Pit Bulls. After surgery these ears tend to bend medially, often lying flat on top of the head. They are difficult to train to stand correctly. A pup who has ears with this tendency should be cropped as early as possible, before the cartilage has begun to stiffen. This will allow maximum time for training and taping the ears into the proper position.

Special Effects

If your new in-laws are visiting and you want Maria to look her very best, a few extras will make her appear especially pert and pretty.

If Maria has cropped ears, use a small scissors with round tips (to protect her eyes in case she moves suddenly) and, starting at the base of the ear, cut the hair along the outer edge of the ear so it is flush with the edge from the base to the tip. Then hold the ear inside out and trim all the fuzzy little hairs inside the ear and at the base of the ear (be careful not to nick the little bumps and ridges). Finally, cut and blend the hair that may stick out in little tufts at the outer edge of the ear.

Pit Bulls wag their tails so hard and bump so many things with them that it's no wonder their tails often look scruffy. If Maria's tail isn't as sleek as the rest of her, hold it either straight up or out and begin by carefully, almost one hair at a time, cutting off the broken or protruding hairs on the underside. Now do the same for each side of the tail, and finally for the top. Does Maria have a funny little curl of hair on the end of her tail? Cut it off and shape the straight hairs just above it to make a neat new tip.

The Inside Outs of Good Looks

Good grooming is no substitute for poor health or lack of physical fitness. Good looks start from within, with quality food, regular exercise, clean housing and no internal or external parasites. Health problems sometimes first show themselves through a dry, brittle coat lacking in luster. Pit Bulls in good condition sparkle from the inside out, and regular grooming sessions simply bring the healthy glow to the surface.

chapter 7

Keeping your
American
Pit Bull Terrier
Healthy

Hearty and robust, with a high tolerance for pain, your American Pit Bull Terrier should seldom show signs of sickness. In fact, if Beau seems to be ill or in pain, it's a good idea to visit your veterinarian immediately. Pit Bulls typically appear brave and strong, and if Beau cannot keep up that pretense, chances are he is quite sick indeed.

With Pit Bulls, many of the most dangerous diseases are preventable through vaccinations, and other problems can be avoided through good nutrition, adequate housing, cleanliness, regular brushing and daily exercise. Next to you and your family, your veterinarian is Beau's best friend. Take Beau to your veterinarian for an examination within two days of bringing him home, whether his next vaccination is due or not.

Visiting the Veterinarian

Feed Beau lightly an hour or more before driving him to the veterinarian, as that may keep him from getting carsick. In any case, pack a roll of paper towels and a container of those wonderful wet wipes used on human babies. Bring along Beau's health record (his breeder should give it to you at the time of purchase), and a stool sample in a plastic baggie. In the veterinarian's office, keep Beau on your lap or in his crate. Do not allow him to play on the floor or sniff strange dogs, because it is easy for young puppies to pick up germs.

Even if thinking about Beau getting a shot makes you nervous, don't let him know that. Be friendly with the veterinarian, not nervous, or Beau will feel your tension and become fearful himself. Hold Beau in place gently for the veterinarian's examination, but as firmly as necessary. Talk to him in a happy, upbeat way, because if you console or coddle him, he'll be certain something terrible is going to happen. Beau will take his cues from you. If he senses that you like your veterinarian, he will like your veterinarian.

Vital Vaccinations

When you bought Beau, you should have received a list of his inoculations (shots) and his worming schedule, complete with dates. This is the health record that you should show your veterinarian so he or she can plan future treatments. The shots your veterinarian will schedule are the best preventive measure possible to keep Beau from contracting a variety of potentially fatal diseases. The number and type of inoculations your veterinarian selects may depend upon your locale. If you plan to travel a lot with Beau, tell your veterinarian, because exposure to strange dogs and new places may demand extra precautions. Don't take Beau on any outings until you are sure that his inoculations are complete. Following his puppy series, Beau will need a booster shot every year of his adult life.

Combination shots have various names depending on the company that made them, but their names are usually made up of letters, such as DHLPP. This is what the letters stand for, and why these shots are so essential:

A FIRST-AID KIT

Keep a canine first-aid kit on hand for general care and emergencies. Check it periodically to make sure liquids haven't spilled or dried up, and replace medications and materials after they're used. Your kit should include:

Activated charcoal tablets

Adhesive tape
(1 and 2 inches wide)

Antibacterial ointment
(for skin and eyes)

Aspirin (buffered or enteric coated, *not* Ibuprofen)

Bandages: Gauze rolls (1 and 2 inches wide) and dressing pads

Cotton balls

Diarrhea medicine

Dosing syringe

Hydrogen peroxide (3%)

Petroleum jelly

Rectal thermometer

Rubber gloves

Rubbing alcohol

Scissors

Tourniquet

Towel

Tweezers

D is for Distemper: Distemper is the number-one killer of unvaccinated dogs and spreads rapidly from one dog to another. Its victims are usually puppies, although older dogs may contract it, too. Because distemper shows up in various forms, it is sometimes difficult for even experienced veterinarians to diagnose. While dogs with distemper occasionally recover, they often suffer permanent damage to their brain or nervous system. Symptoms of distemper include diarrhea, vomiting, reduced appetite, cough, nasal discharge, inflamed eyes, fever, exhaustion and lack of interest in toys or games. If you ever think your puppy has come down with distemper, take him to your veterinarian immediately. Dogs who receive treatment early have a better chance of survival.

H is for Hepatitis: Infectious hepatitis in dogs is not transmissible to humans, although it affects the liver just as it does in humans. In dogs, it spreads through contact with an infected dog's stool, urine or saliva. One specific symptom is intense thirst, but all the other symptoms are similar to those of distemper. The disease progresses rapidly and is often fatal, so prompt veterinary treatment is critical.

L is for Leptospirosis: Leptospirosis is caused by a spirochete, a microorganism which is often carried by rats. It can infect a dog who has contact with a rat or eats something contaminated by rats. Symptoms include bloody diarrhea or urine, fever, depression, red and congested eyes and mouth membranes, painful mouth ulcers, vomiting, increased thirst, loss of appetite and pain when moving. The whites of the eyes may become red or jaundiced. The dog's kidneys and liver can be permanently damaged, so quick veterinary treatment is essential. Since humans can contract lepto, it's important to carefully prevent infecting yourself when caring for a sick dog. Your veterinarian will explain the proper precautions.

P is for Parvovirus: Parvovirus is a deadly killer that was unknown in dogs until 1977. It is believed to be a strain of feline distemper that mutated to infect dogs. The virus attacks the stomach lining, bone marrow and lymph nodes, and in young puppies, the heart. It spreads rapidly from dog to dog through contaminated stools, easily carried here and there via dog paws or shoes. Beginning with depression and a loss of appetite, symptoms soon progress to vomiting, diarrhea (sometimes bloody) and fever. Puppies with infected hearts (myocardial parvovirus) often die suddenly or within one or two days of contracting the disease. Those few who recover may develop chronic heart problems later. How severely adult dogs are affected depends upon the individual dog. Some become violently ill, while others just lose their appetite for a day or two.

P is also for Parainfluenza: Parainfluenza has a couple of other names. Veterinarians may refer to it as infectious canine tracheobronchitis, while its common name is kennel cough. Highly contagious from dog to dog, parainfluenza is caused by several different viruses as well as a bacterium. Symptoms are a frequent dry, hacking cough and sometimes a nasal discharge. Other than that, the dog usually appears to feel fine, and many dogs infected with kennel cough don't even miss a meal. Dogs vaccinated against parainfluenza sometimes come down with it anyway, but usually have milder symptoms than unvaccinated dogs. While the disease usually runs its course, kennel cough is more dangerous to puppies than it is to adult dogs. They should be kept in a warm, humid room while recovering. For dogs of all ages, your veterinarian may prescribe antibiotics to prevent complications and medication to control coughing.

Rabies: Rabies is always fatal, and a dog with rabies is a danger to humans and other animals. The disease is

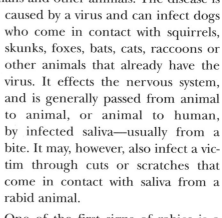

caused by a virus and can infect dogs who come in contact with squirrels, skunks, foxes, bats, cats, raccoons or other animals that already have the virus. It effects the nervous system, and is generally passed from animal to animal, or animal to human, by infected saliva—usually from a bite. It may, however, also infect a victim through cuts or scratches that come in contact with saliva from a rabid animal.

One of the first signs of rabies is a change in disposition. A gentle dog may show signs of aggression, or an independent dog may suddenly crave affection. Soon the dog's pupils may

Use tweezers to remove ticks from your dog.

become dilated, and light may appear to cause him pain. Eventually the dog will want no attention or petting at all, and may show signs of stomach trouble and a fever. Later symptoms can include lack of coordination, random biting, bared teeth, twitching facial muscles, or loss of control of the facial muscles, resulting in an open mouth with the tongue hanging out. The dog's voice may change and he may drool, paw at his mouth and cough. Eventually he slips into a coma and dies. All warmblooded animals are subject to the disease, so anyone bitten by a dog (or any other animal) should see a doctor right away.

The rabies vaccine prevents this dreaded disease. Your veterinarian will give the rabies shot separately, not in combination with the other vaccines. Some rabies shots are good for longer than a year, so ask your veterinarian when your dog's shot should be renewed.

After that list of gloom and doom, how about a cheerful reminder? Preventive medicine can keep your beloved Beau safe from all these deadly diseases. Just follow the vaccination schedule your veterinarian recommends.

Worm Control

Besides vaccinating to prevent contagious diseases, your veterinarian should also check Beau for internal parasites, such as intestinal worms and heartworms. Your veterinarian will need a sample of Beau's stool to check for **roundworms**, **whipworms**, **tapeworms** and **hookworms**, while a blood test is necessary to detect **heartworms**. No matter how carefully you care for Beau, he can still become infested with all of the worms except heartworm. Well-cared-for dogs shouldn't get heartworm, because their owners give them the preventive medication prescribed by their veterinarian.

Common internal parasites (l-r): roundworm, whipworm, tapeworm and hookworm.

The symptoms of roundworms, whipworms, tapeworms and hookworms are all similar, and include a rough, dry coat, dull eyes, a generally unsound appearance, weakness, weight loss despite an enormous appetite, coughing, vomiting, diarrhea, and sometimes, bloody stools. But don't wait for symptoms to show up; few dogs have all of these symptoms, and some dogs lose their appetite entirely when infested with worms. Other dogs show no symptoms at all until they become seriously anemic from a heavy infestation.

Do not be embarrassed if your Pit Bull gets worms. Many puppies are born with roundworms, and dogs can become infested with worms while out for a walk or from biting at a flea. Treatment is not dangerous and it is effective. The important thing is to have your

Living with an
American Pit
Bull Terrier

*These specks in
your dog's fur
mean he has
fleas.*

*Three types of
ticks (l-r): the
wood tick,
brown dog tick
and deer tick.*

veterinarian check your dog's stool at least twice a year, then give your dog the prescribed medication exactly as instructed.

Heartworms are a different story. They are transmitted from dog to dog by the bite of a mosquito, and eight months or more may go by from the time a dog is bitten until the worms mature. Treatment is dangerous (although less dangerous than the deadly worm), but your dog should not have to undergo treatment, because heartworms are preventable. Puppies can be put on preventive medication at a young age and

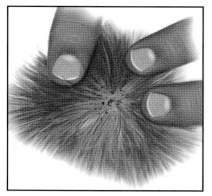

from then on should be tested annually. Because the medication may make a dog who is harboring adult heartworms critically ill, adult dogs must test free of the worms before they can begin a preventive regimen. Symptoms of heartworm infestation include a chronic cough, weight loss and exhaustion, because the worms interfere with the action of the dog's heart. Prevention is the only defense, and it must be started early and continue throughout the dog's life.

Creepy Crawlies—the External Parasites

Fleas, ticks, ear mites and **lice** are all looking for a free lunch and a cozy home, compliments of your Pit Bull. **Deer ticks** are especially dangerous as they may carry

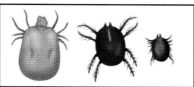

Lyme disease. Symptoms of Lyme disease include fatigue, loss of appetite, fever and sometimes swollen glands in the neck. In areas where the deer tick is prevalent, avoid those wonderful walks in the woods, keep your lawn well-trimmed and take precautions to keep field mice from nesting in your home. Other types of ticks may also be dangerous. **Rocky Mountain spotted fever** can be transmitted by ticks, and tick bites can cause paralysis in dogs. When you visit your veterinarian, ask for preventive suggestions based on your area of the country.

Ticks come in a variety of sizes, and in colors ranging from brown to gray to rather blue. They are fairly easy to see on a Pit Bull because of his short coat. Ticks usually bed down on the dog's head or neck but may be found anywhere on the body. Don't attempt to pull attached ticks off Beau by hand; instead, use a preparation recommended by your veterinarian to safely remove them. If you are camping in the woods far from a veterinary clinic and didn't pack a tick preparation, separate Beau's hair so you can see where the tick has embedded itself in the skin. The embedded part is the tick's head. Then, using a tweezers, clamp down as close to the head as possible and pull it out. If part of the head remains in Beau's skin, apply an antiseptic.

Ear mites live in the ear canal, irritating Beau's sensitive ears and producing a dry, rusty brown to black discharge. See your veterinarian if you suspect ear mites: the condition is easily treatable. Lice seldom bother Pit Bulls, and when they do they can be quickly destroyed with modern preparations. Fleas, on the other hand, are never easy to get rid of. They often become resistant, or actually adapt to insecticides, so new and updated versions of flea dips, powders and sprays appear on the market every year. Your veterinarian knows which preparations work best in your locale, so if your dog or your home is bothered by creepy crawlies, ask for professional help.

FIGHTING FLEAS

Remember, the fleas you see on your dog are only part of the problem—the smallest part! To rid your dog and home of fleas, you need to treat your dog *and* your home. Here's how:

• Identify where your pet(s) sleep. These are "hot spots."

• Clean your pets' bedding regularly by vacuuming and washing.

• Spray "hot spots" with a non-toxic, long-lasting flea larvicide.

• Treat outdoor "hot spots" with insecticide.

• Kill eggs on pets with a product containing insect growth regulators (IGRs).

• Kill fleas on pets per your veterinarian's recommendation.

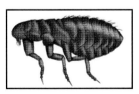

The flea is a die-hard pest.

Potential Problems

Your Pit Bull may never encounter any of the following problems, but it's sensible and safe to be aware of them:

Sarcoptic Mange: Sarcoptic mange is caused by mites. It will make Beau itch, and you will see tiny red bumps and patchy, crusty areas on his body, legs or stomach. Take him to the veterinarian. The condition is treatable and will respond to topical medication.

Follicular Mange: This mange is caused by a different type of mite. Also called demodectic mange or red mange, this condition may or may not make Beau itch. Whether it bothers him or not, you will notice small, circular, moth-eaten-like patches, usually on his head and along his back, sides and neck. Juvenile cases, involving a young dog with only a few patches, might be stress-related. Perhaps Beau recently spent a few days in a boarding kennel. Some females, for example, get a patch or two of mange when they come into season for the first time. Your veterinarian has medication to clear up this condition, but if Beau ever gets a generalized case of this mange (covering much of his body), don't use him for breeding as he could pass the problem on to his young.

Fleabite Allergic Dermatitis: This is an allergic reaction to fleabites. It can occur at any time in your dog's life, sometimes causing an allergic reaction in a dog who didn't previously react to fleabites. Symptoms include intense itching combined with reddened, swollen and hot skin. If Beau becomes allergic to fleabites, he will continuously scratch, lick, and even bite at the affected area. Without treatment, the

---

YOUR PUPPY'S VACCINES

Vaccines are given to prevent your dog from getting an infectious disease like canine distemper or rabies. Vaccines are the ultimate preventive medicine: they're given before your dog ever gets the disease so as to protect him from the disease. That's why it is necessary for your dog to be vaccinated routinely. Puppy vaccines start at eight weeks of age for the five-in-one DHLPP vaccine and are given every three to four weeks until the puppy is sixteen months old. Your veterinarian will put your puppy on a proper schedule and will remind you when to bring in your dog for shots.

area will eventually become dry and scaly, the skin will thicken and the hair will fall out. Prompt veterinary treatment is important to relieve the allergy and prevent secondary infections in the spots where Beau opened his skin in an effort to relieve the itch.

Ringworm: In spite of its name, ringworm is a fungal infection, not a worm. Carried more often by cats than dogs, ringworm causes small, round, itchy bald patches, which are often inflamed because the dog cannot help but scratch them. They are easily cured by the fungicide your veterinarian will recommend.

Just as these skin problems have similar symptoms, so do several others that Beau might encounter. Since it's difficult to determine exactly which condition is making Beau itch, and each one requires a different medication, leave diagnosis and treatment to your veterinarian.

A healthy Pit Bull takes a rest.

Clogged Anal Glands: If Beau is scooting along the floor on his haunches, he probably has clogged anal glands. His anal glands are located on each side of his anus, and they secrete a substance that enables Beau to pass his stool. When clogged, they are extremely uncomfortable, smell bad, and could become infected. Your vet-

erinarian can quickly unclog Beau's anal glands, or you can do it yourself if you are game. Just use one hand to hold his tail up and, with a tissue or soft cloth in your other hand, take the skin on either side of the anus, just below the middle, in your thumb and forefinger. Then push in slightly and squeeze gently. If you succeed, a brownish, nasty-smelling substance will be on your cloth and Beau will stop scooting. Blood or pus in the secretion is a sign of infection, so if either one is present, take Beau to the veterinarian.

Hip Dysplasia: Hip dysplasia is caused by an abnormality of one or both hip joints. If Beau has a borderline case, it may never be noticeable to him or to you, and the only way you would know is by having his hips X-rayed. In more severe cases, HD causes lameness in the hindquarters, ranging in severity from a slightly odd gait to inability to stand. Hip dysplasia is incurable, but there are several ways to lessen its pain, including surgery for some cases. Your veterinarian will have to X-ray Beau to determine the best treatment for him.

All dogs should be X-rayed and certified clear of hip dysplasia by the Orthopedic Foundation for Animals (OFA) before they are used for breeding. Your veterinarian will be able to guide you through the process.

Make a temporary splint by wrapping the leg in firm casing, then bandaging it.

Ruptured Cruciate Ligament: The cruciate ligament is in the stifle joint, and its rupture is similar to the knee injury that puts many top football players on the bench. This condition is an athletic injury that will cause Beau to limp noticeably or even refuse to walk on one of the rear legs. As this injury most often sidelines heavily muscled, extremely active dogs, the Pit Bull's structure and personality combine to make him a prime candidate for the problem. In most cases, a ruptured cruciate ligament must be corrected surgically.

Hypothyroidism: The result of a hormone deficiency, hypothyroidism affects Beau's metabolism. Symptoms include a reduced activity level, in other words, less playing and more sleeping. Eventually Beau will lose interest in family fun and won't seem as bright or alert as before. Beau may either gain or lose weight, and his hair will begin to dry and thin out, especially along his sides and flanks, where bald spots may occur.

Hypothyroidism is controllable in most cases, and with treatment Beau will slowly return to his alert, happy self. Your veterinarian will give him a blood test to confirm the problem and determine proper dosages of daily thyroid hormone.

Calluses: Dogs get calluses on their elbows and sometimes on the outsides of their hocks from sleeping on hard, rough surfaces such as concrete or gravel. The skin of the affected area becomes hairless, gray, thick and wrinkled. Usually calluses only hurt the dog's appearance, but sometimes they fester and evolve into open sores. Deep, soft bedding will prevent calluses and help keep Beau beautiful as well as comfortable.

Handling Common Problems

Loss of Appetite: By itself, with no other symptoms, a brief lack of interest in food is seldom serious. For example, many dogs need less food during the heat of summer and may occasionally leave some, or even all, of their dinner untouched. If Beau misses one meal, don't worry. But if he refuses all food for two days in a row, he should be checked by your veterinarian.

Run your hands regularly over your dog to feel for any injuries.

Visit your veterinarian right away if loss of appetite is accompanied by other symptoms such as diarrhea, obvious pain, lack of interest in household activities, fever or difficulty breathing.

Vomiting: If Beau has no other symptoms of sickness, but vomits once or twice, simply keep a close watch on him. He may be back to normal in no time. A dry, unseasoned cracker, such as a plain saltine, may help.

If Beau vomits three or more times, lacks interest in household activities and appears lethargic, or has symptoms such as frequent diarrhea in addition to vomiting, see your veterinarian the same day.

Diarrhea: At the first sign of diarrhea, remove all food from Beau for twenty-four hours but make sure he has a continuous supply of fresh drinking water. If, after twenty-four hours, Beau has not passed a stool at all or the stool appears firmer, give him a small portion of cooked rice with a bit of boiled chicken or cooked ground beef (without the fat) mixed through it.

Some of the many household substances harmful to your dog.

As the stool continues to normalize, gradually (over a period of three or four days) return Beau to his regular diet. Do this by first mixing rice and meat with a portion of his regular food, and later adding more of his regular food and less rice with each feeding. While Beau is recovering from diarrhea, do not give him any

dairy products or anything fatty. If, after the first twenty-four hours without food, Beau still has diarrhea, or if you see blood in the stool, or he vomits, lacks appetite or has little interest in household activities, see your veterinarian immediately. Take a stool sample with you. To do so, turn a plastic, zip-lock bag inside out and pick up a portion of stool. Turn the bag right side out, close it, and take it to your veterinarian while it is still fresh.

Check your dog's teeth frequently and brush them regularly.

Do not wait twenty-four hours to take Beau to the veterinarian if the diarrhea is severe. He needs immediate treatment if the diarrhea is liquid and has a vile odor, or if he has stomach pain or is straining in addition to the diarrhea.

Lameness (mild): If Beau is lame for no easily apparent reason (check pads for cuts or brush burns) and has no other symptoms (i.e., he still eats well and interacts with the family), wait a day or two before calling the veterinarian. Dogs get bruises, strains and sprains just as people do and often heal quickly. Also, use common sense. Before walking Beau in the heat of summer, check the temperature of the sidewalk. It may be unbearable. In the winter, dogs often act as if they were lame when snow or ice builds up between their pads.

Coughing: A persistent cough signals the possibility of a respiratory infection and should be treated by your veterinarian.

Handy How-To's

All of these tasks are easier to perform if you have a helper.

Taking a Temperature

1. Smear Vaseline about two inches high on a rectal therometer and shake the mercury down.
2. Lift Beau's tail, and gently but firmly push about two inches of the thermometer into his anus.
3. With a soothing voice and firm hands, keep Beau standing steady for about a minute and a half.
4. Withdraw the thermometer, wipe it with tissue so it is easier to see the numbers, and take the reading.
5. Wash the thermometer with disinfectant before storing it for future use.

Normal temperature for a dog ranges between 100 degrees Fahrenheit and 102 degrees Fahrenheit. If Beau's temperature is either higher or lower than that, consult your veterinarian. The exception is a female close to giving birth. A drop in body temperature to below 100 degrees indicates that the female will go into labor within twenty-four to thirty-six hours.

Giving a Pill

When your veterinarian prescribes pills that aren't the delicious chewable variety, the easiest method of giving them is by hiding them in a bit of cheese, peanut butter or some other soft treat with a strong odor. If Beau catches on to the deception and refuses the treat, or eats the treat but leaves the pill, you will have to resort to the following method:

1. Place one hand on Beau's muzzle with your fingers pointing toward his nose, thumb on one side and fingers on the other.

2. Tilt Beau's head back so he is looking up, and squeeze inward and upward with your thumb and fingers. This will make him open his mouth, and he will not want to close it because his lips are positioned between his own teeth.

3. Hold the pill in your right hand between your thumb and index finger. Use your free fingers to push downward on Beau's lower jaw, and place the pill as far back on the top side of his tongue as you can with your index finger.

To give a pill, open the mouth wide, then drop it in the back of the throat.

4. Close Beau's mouth and hold it shut by keeping your left hand around his muzzle. His nose should

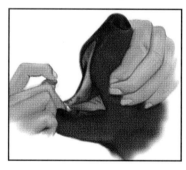

still be pointing slightly upward. With your right hand, stroke Beau's throat (from behind the chin to his upper chest) and tell him what a good boy he is. Continue until you see or feel him swallow. Many dogs try to stick out their tongue immediately after they swallow, so that is a good clue that you succeeded in medicating your dog.

5. Never give Beau a pill unless it was prescribed or approved by your veterinarian. Something as simple as an aspirin substitute can be harmful, and even fatal, to dogs.

GIVING LIQUID MEDICATION

1. Put the prescribed amount of liquid medication in an eye dropper or syringe (without a needle).

2. Tilt Beau's head back so that he is looking upward.

3. Place your finger inside the corner of Beau's mouth and gently stretch his cheek outward to form a pocket.

4. Drip the medication into the pocket slowly, giving Beau time to swallow.

APPLYING EYE DROPS

1. Tilt Beau's head back so that he is looking upward.

2. Using your thumb and index finger, gently hold his eyelids open.

3. Drop the prescribed number of drops directly on the eyeball, unless your veterinarian or the label directs otherwise.

4. Keep Beau's head tilted upward for a minimum of ten seconds so that the drops don't roll out before they have any effect.

APPLYING EYE OINTMENT

1. Tilt Beau's head back so that he is looking upward.

Squeeze eye ointment into the lower lid.

2. Gently pull Beau's lower eyelid down and place a line of ointment inside the pocket between the eye and the lid.

3. Close Beau's eye and gently hold it shut for a few seconds.

APPLYING EAR DROPS

1. Gently pull the tip of Beau's ear across his head toward his other ear, so you can easily see the ear canal.

2. Squeeze the prescribed number of drops into the ear canal.

3. While still firmly holding Beau's head (he may shake his head and send the drops in all directions), massage the area just below the ear for several seconds.

CHECKING BEAU'S PULSE (HEARTBEAT)

The pulse indicates the circulation of blood and expresses the working of the heart. It should be checked when Beau is calm, not immediately following heavy exercise.

To find Beau's pulse, place your index or middle finger on the inside of his thigh near the groin area and probe gently until you locate the artery just under the skin where the pulse is obvious. Check your watch and carefully count the pulse for exactly one minute. Another viable method with a shorthaired dog such as the Pit Bull is to simply feel or watch the heart beat and count the beats for exactly one minute. The heartbeat can be felt or even seen as a slight, even movement of the chest on the dog's left side just behind the elbow (the location of the heart).

The normal pulse for a dog is between 80 and 120 beats per minute, depending on such variables as age and weight. If Beau is not within that range, have him checked by your veterinarian.

WHEN TO CALL THE VET

In any emergency situation, you should call your veterinarian immediately. You can make the difference in your dog's life by staying as calm as possible when you call and by giving the doctor or the assistant as much information as possible before you leave for the clinic. That way, the vet will be able to take immediate, specific action to remedy your dog's situation.

Emergencies include acute abdominal pain, suspected poisoning, snakebite, burns, frostbite, shock, dehydration, abnormal vomiting or bleeding, and deep wounds. You are the best judge of your dog's health, as you live with and observe him every day. Don't hesitate to call your veterinarian if you suspect trouble.

Emergency How-To's

Muzzling: Even the sweetest, most loving dog may try to bite when in pain. Using a muzzle is the quickest, safest and most humane way to keep from being bitten when handling an injured dog.

1. Use a piece of soft material such as a nylon stocking, necktie, or strip from a tee shirt, and talk soothingly to Beau while applying the muzzle.

2. Holding the material with one end in each hand, make a loop and close it with a half-knot.

3. Slip the loop around Beau's muzzle and draw it tight with the half-knot on top.

4. Make a second loop around the muzzle, this time tying the half-knot under Beau's bottom jaw.

5. Finish the emergency muzzle by bringing the two ends (one on each side) to the top of Beau's neck. Then tie the ends of the material together in a tight bow on top of his head, just behind the ears.

Severe Lameness (possible fracture) and How To Transport: Signs of a broken bone (fracture) are holding the injured leg up off the ground, pain, swelling, a dangling or severely swollen leg, no use of the hind legs or the dog's inability to move the injured leg. If you suspect that lameness is due to a fracture, take Beau to your veterinarian immediately. Put a muzzle on him first, then move him carefully, trying not to aggravate the injured limb. To do this, place a blanket or other strong piece of material on the ground beside Beau and gently, by the scruff of the neck, pull him onto the blanket. Two people (one at each end) can lift the blanket to put Beau in the car for transport to the veterinarian.

Use a scarf or old hose to make a temporary muzzle, as shown.

Other causes of lameness that require veterinary attention are a deep cut that may need stitches, or a puncture wound. In either case, Beau must be treated to avoid infection.

Heatstroke: If Beau suffers a heatstroke, he must have immediate attention. Sometimes only a cold-water enema applied by a veterinarian will save him. Symptoms include some, but usually not all, of the following:

- Rapid or heavy breathing with the mouth and tongue a very bright red.

- Thick saliva.

- Vomiting.

- Bloody diarrhea.

- Unsteadiness on his feet, and possibly falling.

- A hot, dry nose with legs and ears hot to the touch.

- In extreme cases the dog may be glassy-eyed and his lips may appear gray.

Always keep your veterinarian's number handy.

When a dog's rectal temperature is 104 degrees or more, he is in serious trouble. If you suspect heatstroke, immediately take Beau somewhere cooler, and wet him down gradually with cool (not ice cold) water. Give him cool water to drink, but in small amounts at a time, never all at once. Apply cold compresses to his belly and groin area, but do not suddenly put your over-heated dog into extremely cold water. While cooling Beau, make preparations to get him to your veterinarian.

Be especially cautious if Beau has already suffered a heatstroke and survived. After a dog has one such stroke, he seems to be more prone to getting another.

Snakebite: Symptoms include swelling, labored breathing, glazed eyes and drooling. The best first aid you can give while rushing Beau to your veterinarian is to keep him warm and as calm and inactive as possible.

Shock: Shock is a potential result of severe trauma such as loss of blood, poisoning, second- and third-degree burns, serious infection or dehydration, and is most often seen in accident cases. Best described as a state of collapse, shock can range from mild to life-threatening.

A dog in shock has a glassy-eyed appearance; takes quick, shallow breaths; has a rapid, weak pulse; a low body temperature (is cold to the touch); appears weak (usually lies down); and has pale gums. If you suspect that Beau is in shock, keep him warm by covering him with a blanket, towel or jacket, and talk soothingly to keep him as calm as possible. Control any bleeding (see below) and take him to the nearest veterinarian immediately.

BLEEDING DO'S AND DON'TS:

If Beau is bleeding, **Do**:

- Remain calm so you can think and so Beau doesn't panic and bleed even faster.
- Keep Beau still by holding him firmly and talking soothingly.
- Put pressure directly on the wound with a clean cloth. If one is not handy, use your fingers or hand. Applying pressure to the two edges of a wound, with your thumb on one side and your index finger on the other, often slows the flow.
- Put a clean gauze pad on the wound and apply pressure with your hand or fingers. After ten to fifteen seconds, remove the pad carefully to see if the bleeding slowed or stopped. If the wound is still bleeding slowly, or begins to bleed again after stopping, reapply the gauze pad and the pressure for about twenty seconds.
- If Beau is bleeding from a wound you can't reach with pressure (such as a nosebleed), put an icepack (ice in a cloth or towel) on the area.
- Take Beau to the veterinarian so the wound will be properly cleaned, and stitched if necessary.

Familiarize yourself with how your dog looks and feels when he is healthy so you can easily spot when he is unhealthy.

If Beau is bleeding heavily, **Do**:

- Put a clean gauze pad on the wound and put firm pressure on the pad for thirty seconds with your fingers or hand. If the blood is bright red and spurting, use heavy pressure.

- Wrap a three-inch-wide adhesive bandage firmly (or tightly if blood is spurting) over the gauze pad. This is called a pressure bandage. If blood comes through the bandage, do not remove it, but put another tighter bandage on top of it.

- Keeping Beau as still as possible, wrap him in a blanket and go straight to the nearest veterinarian.

If Beau is bleeding:

- **Do not** hestitate to act, or panic.

- **Do not** move him more than necessary or excite him.

- **Do not** use a wiping or dabbing motion on the wound. That usually makes it bleed harder.

- **Do not** clean the wound. Attempting to clean a wound before the bleeding stops promotes more bleeding.

- **Do not** try to apply a tourniquet. Applied by an amateur, a tourniquet may cause more problems than it corrects.

- **Do not** leave a pressure bandage on for longer than thirty minutes without making sure it isn't too tight. To check for tightness, look at the limb below the bandage. If it is swollen or cold, or if a conscious dog shows no reaction to pain when the skin below the bandage is pinched, loosen the pressure and reapply the bandage a little less firmly.

Choking: Signs of choking are saliva dripping, using the front paws to claw at the mouth, trying to vomit, or an open mouth that the dog seems unable to close.

If Beau has one or more of the above symptoms but is still somewhat able to breathe, take him to the veterinarian right away. If Beau's tongue is turning blue and he seems close to passing out, wedge an item, such as one end of a tightly rolled-up newspaper section or magazine, between his upper and lower back teeth on only one side of his mouth. This will keep his mouth open so you can see in. Check the roof of his mouth, the back of his throat and between his teeth for

the item causing the obstruction. Taking care not to be bitten, check the back of Beau's tongue by pulling the tongue forward and a few inches out of his mouth. When you discover the object causing the problem, pull it out with your fingers or with a long-nosed pliers.

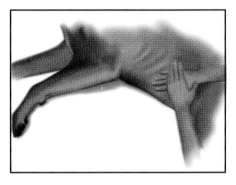

As a last resort, if the object is lodged so that you cannot remove it, lift Beau by the hind legs so his head is dangling toward the floor and shake him hard. This may loosen the object and clear the airway. If Beau is not breathing after the obstruction is removed, give mouth-to-nose resuscitation.

Applying abdominal thrusts can save a choking dog.

Mouth-to-Nose Resuscitation: If Beau stops breathing, first check to see if a foreign body is obstructing his airway (see "Choking" above). To give mouth-to-nose resuscitation:

- Put Beau into position by lying him on his right side. His head should be back and his mouth must be closed.

- Using one hand to hold Beau's mouth shut, place your mouth over his nose and breath into it deeply about six times. (If working on a little puppy, use quick, shallow breaths).

- Beau may begin breathing again after the first six breaths. If he does, keep a careful watch on him for the next several hours.

- If Beau does not resume breathing right away, continue with mouth-to-nose at a speed of about twenty breaths per minute or one breath every three seconds. Continue until Beau breathes on his own, and then watch him carefully while taking him to the veterinarian.

- If after ten minutes Beau is not breathing on his own, his gums and tongue are blue, his pupils are dilated and he doesn't blink when you touch his open eye, he is probably dead.

Stings: Signs that Beau was stung by a bee or bitten by a spider or other insect include a sudden yelp of pain, welts, sometimes additional swelling, and frantically biting at or scratching the area of the sting(s).

It may be enough to check the area of pain and, if a stinger is present, to remove it with tweezers. Then hold a cold compress to the area or use a soothing lotion formulated for humans, such as calamine. If there is considerable swelling, or if Beau appears to be in pain or in shock, take him to the veterinarian immediately.

Don't listen to the myths about spaying and neutering. It is essential for a happy, healthy pet.

Spaying and Neutering for a Healthier, Happier Dog

The nicest thing you can do for yourself, your family and your Pit Bull is to have your dog spayed or neutered. Females spayed before their first season, usually at around six months of age, are at much less risk of developing breast cancer than unspayed females. Because spaying removes the female's reproductive organs, spayed females never suffer cancers or infections of the ovaries or uterus. In addition, they don't have unwanted pregnancies and won't bleed all over your rug for several days twice a year.

Spayed females are also nicer to live with. They won't entice males to sing in chorus on your front lawn, and they won't suddenly develop a desire to roam. Spaying helps a female's disposition remain consistent, and lets her take part in competitive performance events, such as obedience or weight pulling, without a three-week break every six months. In short, spaying a female when she is young gives her a healthier life, gives you fewer hassles, and doesn't add to the pet overpopulation problem.

Keeping your male dog intact for breeding purposes, either because you believe you are being kind to him or because someone with a female may seek him out for stud service, also does your dog and you an injustice. Neutering a male dog before he is a year old could save him the pain of prostate problems, including cancer, when he ages. It will also make him easier to live with.

An Elizabethan collar keeps your dog from licking a fresh wound.

Male hormones make dogs desire every female in season whose scent wafts by on the wind, and some of them break doors, windows and fences to find the female. Male hormones also make dogs more aggressive toward other dogs, and sometimes contribute to housebreaking problems, as with scent marking (when the male lifts his leg and urinates on objects inside the home to stake out his territory). Sexual frustration (caused by male hormones) is what makes a dog embarrass his owner by making love to the boss's leg during a dinner party. While neutering won't immediately cure a frustrated, dog-aggressive, escape artist with a housebreaking problem, it eliminates the production of male hormone and almost always starts him on the road to improvement.

Dog shows are a showcase for breeding stock, so spayed and neutered animals are not permitted to compete in conformation. If a show career is in your puppy's future, refrain from spaying or neutering until your dog retires from competition. Even if your dog wins a championship and you decide to use him for breeding, spaying or neutering following your dog's breeding career will give him a longer, healthier life.

MYTHS, LIES AND CARTOONS

It is a myth that spaying or neutering makes a dog fat and lazy. Overfeeding and lack of exercise do that. In fact, spayed and neutered pets are often the best performers in obedience, agility, and other competitive events. Neutered males can consistently keep their mind on their work, and spayed females can compete throughout the year without losing six to eight weeks when in season. Nearly all service dogs (guide dogs for the blind or deaf, and dogs who help the physically handicapped) are spayed or neutered.

It is untrue that neutered males don't make good guardians. Not only will they loyally protect their homes and families, but they concentrate on their job better then males who have the scent of a female on their mind. Spayed females are also reliable guardians.

Cartoonists and comedians often get laughs by implying that male dogs think like humans and are sad or resentful about being "castrated." While such skits are funny at the Comedy Club, the concept is absolutely ridiculous in real life. Dogs don't have human feelings about romantic love and sex. Dogs don't miss the hormones that frustrated them and drove them to get into trouble. In fact, after they are neutered, most dogs become closer to their family, where they really want to be.

The Female Heat Cycle

Unspayed female Pit Bulls usually come into season (heat) twice a year at roughly six-month intervals. They start when they are between six and twelve months old and continue all their lives. The heat usually lasts from eighteen to twenty-one days, and its first sign is a noticeable swelling of the vulva, followed by bleeding (showing color). Males are often attracted to a female at this early stage, but she usually wants nothing to do with them and either sits down when they try to mount her or fights them off. After seven to nine days, the bloody discharge changes to cream or straw-colored, signaling the second stage of heat. The female's attitude often changes, too, and she may become friendly and inviting toward males. It is during this stage, which usually lasts from the tenth to the fifteenth day, that the female is ovulating and can become pregnant. The final stage of heat often continues until the twenty-first day or longer. During this period the female is still attractive to males, but she usually wants nothing more to do with them.

When a female is in season, it is impossible to be too careful. Not every female's cycle or behavior is the same, and some may be agreeable to breeding much earlier or much later than the norm. Since males are attracted to your door from the first swelling of the vulva until nature washes the scent of season from your yard, it is important to keep your female securely confined during her entire heat cycle. Females in heat have made escapes that the great Houdini would admire, and male dogs will do whatever it takes to woo your female, including digging under and climbing over the fence.

If you breed your female on purpose, it's still necessary to confine her. Female dogs can give birth to puppies from two or more sires in one litter. You may

IDENTIFYING YOUR DOG

It's a terrible thing to think about, but your dog could somehow, someday, get lost or stolen. How would you get him back? Your best bet would be to have some form of identification on your dog. You can choose from a collar and tags, a tattoo, a microchip or a combination of these three.

Every dog should wear a buckle collar with identification tags. They are the quickest and easiest way for a stranger to identify your dog. It's best to inscribe the tags with your name and phone number; you don't need to include your dog's name.

There are two ways to permanently identify your dog. The first is a tattoo, placed on the inside of your dog's thigh. The tattoo should be your social security number or your dog's AKC registration number.

The second is a microchip, a rice-sized pellet that's inserted under the dog's skin at the base of the neck, between the shoulder blades. When a scanner is passed over the dog, it will beep, notifying the person that the dog has a chip. The scanner will then show a code, identifying the dog. Microchips are becoming more and more popular and are certainly the wave of the future.

have bred Maria to the best American Pit Bull Terrier you could find, but if Bobbie Boxer climbed your fence, some of Maria's puppies may be pure Pit Bulls while others may be mongrels or Pit Boxers!

Sexual Characteristics of the Male

From the time a male Pit Bull is around eight months old, until he is too old to stand up without help, he will probably be willing to breed a female in heat. But stud dogs should never be expected to "perform" outside on hot, muggy days, because even if they succeed, they may still fail because extreme heat kills sperm. It's best to keep a stud dog in the shade, or even in air conditioning, for several hours before he is used, as well as during the actual mating.

Although Pit Bulls of both sexes should be certified clear of heredity defects before they are used for breeding, a defect called orchidism is seen only in the male and can be easily detected by the owner. Orchidism means the dog's testicle(s) did not descend into the scrotum. It is called cryptorchidism when it affects both testicles, and monorchidism when it affects one. Some dogs with orchidism are capable of fathering puppies, but they should never be allowed to do so as they often pass the defect to their young. In fact, dogs with this defect should always be neutered because the undescended testicle(s) may become cancerous.

If you have a young male puppy with undescended testicles, don't panic too soon. Sometimes puppies' testicles do not fully descend until the dog reaches four to five months of age. Also, when the testicles begin to descend, one or both of them may appear one day and disappear the next, only to emerge for good a few days later.

Your Happy, Healthy Pet

Your Dog's Name _____

Name on Your Dog's Pedigree (if your dog has one) _____

_____

Where Your Dog Came From _____

_____

Your Dog's Birthday _____

Your Dog's Veterinarian

    Name _____

    Address _____

    Phone Number_____

    Emergency Number_____

Your Dog's Health

    Vaccines

        type _____ date given _____

        type _____ date given _____

        type _____ date given _____

        type _____ date given _____

    Heartworm

        date tested _____ type used_____ start date _____

Your Dog's License Number_____

Groomer's Name and Number _____

Dogsitter/Walker's Name and Number_____

Awards Your Dog Has Won

    Award _____ date earned _____

    Award _____ date earned _____

part three

Enjoying
your
Dog

chapter 8

Basic
Training

by Ian Dunbar, Ph.D., MRCVS

Training is the jewel in the crown—the most important aspect of doggy husbandry. There is no more important variable influencing dog behavior and temperament than the dog's education: A well-trained, well-behaved and good-natured puppydog is always a joy to live with, but an untrained and uncivilized dog can be a perpetual nightmare. Moreover, deny the dog an education and she will not have the opportunity to fulfill her own canine potential; neither will she have the ability to communicate effectively with her human companions.

Luckily, modern psychological training methods are easy, efficient, effective and, above all, considerably dog-friendly and user-friendly.

Doggy education is as simple as it is enjoyable. But before you can have a good time play-training with your new dog, you have to learn what to do and how to do it. There is no bigger variable influencing the success of dog training than the *owner's* experience and expertise. *Before you embark on the dog's education, you must first educate yourself.*

Basic Training for Owners

Ideally, basic owner training should begin well *before* you select your dog. Find out all you can about your chosen breed first, then master rudimentary training and handling skills. If you already have your puppy-dog, owner training is a dire emergency—the clock is ticking! Especially for puppies, the first few weeks at home are the most important and influential days in the dog's life. Indeed, the cause of most adolescent and adult problems may be traced back to the initial days the pup explores her new home. This is the time to establish the *status quo*—to teach the puppydog how you would like her to behave and so prevent otherwise quite predictable problems.

In addition to consulting breeders and breed books such as this one (which understandably have a positive breed bias), seek out as many pet owners with your breed as you can find. Good points are obvious. What you want to find out are the breed-specific *problems,* so you can nip them in the bud. In particular, you should talk to owners with *adolescent* dogs and make a list of all anticipated problems. Most important, *test drive* at least half a dozen adolescent and adult dogs of your breed yourself. An 8-week-old puppy is deceptively easy to handle, but she will acquire adult size, speed and strength in just four months, so you should learn now what to prepare for.

Puppy and pet dog training classes offer a convenient venue to locate pet owners and observe dogs in action. For a list of suitable trainers in your area, contact the Association of Pet Dog Trainers (see chapter 13). You may also begin your basic owner training by observing other owners in class. Watch as many classes and test drive as many dogs as possible. Select an upbeat, dog-friendly, people-friendly, fun-and-games, puppydog pet training class to learn the ropes. Also, watch training videos and read training books. You must find out what to do and how to do it *before* you have to do it.

Principles of Training

Most people think training comprises teaching the dog to do things such as sit, speak and roll over, but even a 4-week-old pup knows how to do these things already. Instead, the first step in training involves teaching the dog human words for each dog behavior and activity and for each aspect of the dog's environment. That way you, the owner, can more easily participate in the dog's domestic education by directing her to perform specific actions appropriately, that is, at the right time, in the right place and so on. Training opens communication channels, enabling an educated dog to at least understand her owner's requests.

In addition to teaching a dog *what* we want her to do, it is also necessary to teach her *why* she should do what we ask. Indeed, 95 percent of training revolves around motivating the dog *to want to do* what we want. Dogs often understand what their owners want; they just don't see the point of doing it—especially when the owner's repetitively boring and seemingly senseless instructions are totally at odds with much more pressing and exciting doggy distractions. It is not so much the dog that is being stubborn or dominant; rather, it is the owner who has failed to acknowledge the dog's needs and feelings and to approach training from the dog's point of view.

THE MEANING OF INSTRUCTIONS

The secret to successful training is learning how to use training lures to predict or prompt specific behaviors—to coax the dog to do what you want *when* you want. Any highly valued object (such as a treat or toy) may be used as a lure, which the dog will follow with her eyes and nose. Moving the lure in specific ways entices the dog to move her nose, head and entire body in specific ways. In fact, by learning the art of manipulating various lures, it is possible to teach the dog to assume virtually any body position and perform any action. Once you have control over the expression of the dog's behaviors and can elicit any body position or behavior at will, you can easily teach the dog to perform on request.

Teach your dog words for each activity she needs to know, like down.

Tell your dog what you want her to do, use a lure to entice her to respond correctly, then profusely praise and maybe reward her once she performs the desired action. For example, verbally request "Tina, sit!" while you move a squeaky toy upwards and backwards over the dog's muzzle (lure-movement and hand signal), smile knowingly as she looks up (to follow the lure) and sits down (as a result of canine anatomical engineering), then praise her to distraction ("Gooood Tina!"). Squeak the toy, offer a training treat and give your dog and yourself a pat on the back.

Being able to elicit desired responses over and over enables the owner to reward the dog over and over. Consequently, the dog begins to think training is fun. For example, the more the dog is rewarded for sitting, the more she enjoys sitting. Eventually the dog comes to realize that, whereas most sitting is appreciated, sitting immediately upon request usually prompts especially enthusiastic praise and a slew of high-level rewards. The dog begins to sit on cue much of the time, showing that she is starting to grasp the meaning of the owner's verbal request and hand signal.

WHY COMPLY?

Most dogs enjoy initial lure-reward training and are only too happy to comply with their owners' wishes. Unfortunately, repetitive drilling without appreciative feedback tends to diminish the dog's enthusiasm until she eventually fails to see the point of complying anymore. Moreover, as the dog approaches adolescence she becomes more easily distracted as she develops other interests. Lengthy sessions with repetitive exercises tend to bore and demotivate both parties. If it's not fun, the owner doesn't do it and neither does the dog.

Integrate training into your dog's life: The greater number of training sessions each day and the *shorter* they are, the more willingly compliant your dog will

become. Make sure to have a short (just a few seconds) training interlude before every enjoyable canine activity. For example, ask your dog to sit to greet people, to sit before you throw her Frisbee and to sit for her supper. Really, sitting is no different from a canine "Please."

To train your dog, you need gentle hands, a loving heart and a good attitude.

Also, include numerous short training interludes during every enjoyable canine pastime, for example, when playing with the dog or when she is running in the park. In this fashion, doggy distractions may be effectively converted into rewards for training. Just as all games have rules, fun becomes training . . . and training becomes fun.

Eventually, rewards actually become unnecessary to continue motivating your dog. If trained with consideration and kindness, performing the desired behaviors will become self-rewarding and, in a sense, your dog will motivate herself. Just as it is not necessary to reward a human companion during an enjoyable walk in the park, or following a game of tennis, it is hardly necessary to reward our best friend—the dog—for walking by our side or while playing fetch. Human company during enjoyable activities is reward enough for most dogs.

Even though your dog has become self-motivating, it's still good to praise and pet her a lot and offer rewards once in a while, especially for a good job well done. And if for no other reason, praising and rewarding others is good for the human heart.

PUNISHMENT

Without a doubt, lure-reward training is by far the best way to teach: Entice your dog to do what you want and then reward her for doing so. Unfortunately, a human shortcoming is to take the good for granted and to moan and groan at the bad. Specifically, the dog's many good behaviors are ignored while the owner focuses on punishing the dog for making mistakes. In extreme cases, instruction is *limited* to punishing mistakes made by a trainee dog, child, employee or husband, even though it has been proven punishment training is notoriously inefficient and ineffective and is decidedly unfriendly and combative. It teaches the dog that training is a drag, almost as quickly as it teaches the dog to dislike her trainer. Why treat our best friends like our worst enemies?

Punishment training is also much more laborious and time consuming. Whereas it takes only a finite amount of time to teach a dog what to chew, for example, it takes much, much longer to punish the dog for each and every mistake. Remember, *there is only one right way!* So why not teach that right way from the outset?!

To make matters worse, punishment training causes severe lapses in the dog's reliability. Since it is obviously impossible to punish the dog each and every time she misbehaves, the dog quickly learns to distinguish between those times when she must comply (so as to avoid impending punishment) and those times when she need not comply, because punishment is impossible. Such times include when the dog is off leash and 6 feet away, when the owner is otherwise engaged (talking to a friend, watching television, taking a shower, tending to the baby or chatting on the telephone) or when the dog is left at home alone.

Instances of misbehavior will be numerous when the owner is away, because even when the dog complied in the owner's looming presence, she did so unwillingly. The dog was forced to act against her will, rather than molding her will to want to please. Hence, when the owner is absent, not only does the dog know she need not comply, she simply does not want to. Again, the trainee is not a stubborn vindictive beast, but rather the trainer has failed to teach. Punishment training invariably creates unpredictable Jekyll and Hyde behavior.

Trainer's Tools

Many training books extol the virtues of a vast array of training paraphernalia and electronic and metallic gizmos, most of which are designed for canine restraint, correction and punishment, rather than for actual facilitation of doggy education. In reality, most effective training tools are not found in stores; they come from within ourselves. In addition to a willing dog, all you really need is a functional human brain, gentle hands, a loving heart and a good attitude.

In terms of equipment, all dogs do require a quality buckle collar to sport dog tags and to attach the leash (for safety and to comply with local leash laws). Hollow chew toys (like Kongs or sterilized longbones) and a dog bed or collapsible crate are musts for housetraining. Three additional tools are required:

1. specific lures (training treats and toys) to predict and prompt specific desired behaviors;

2. rewards (praise, affection, training treats and toys) to reinforce for the dog what a lot of fun it all is; and

3. knowledge—how to convert the dog's favorite activities and games (potential distractions to training) into "life-rewards," which may be employed to facilitate training.

The most powerful of these is *knowledge*. Education is the key! Watch training classes, participate in training classes, watch videos, read books, enjoy play-training with your dog and then your dog will say "Please," and your dog will say "Thank you!"

Housetraining

If dogs were left to their own devices, certainly they would chew, dig and bark for entertainment and then no doubt highlight a few areas of their living space with sprinkles of urine, in much the same way we decorate by hanging pictures. Consequently, when we ask a dog to live with us, we must teach her *where* she may dig, *where* she may perform her toilet duties, *what* she may chew and *when* she may bark. After all, when left at home alone for many hours, we cannot expect the dog to amuse herself by completing crosswords or watching the soaps on TV!

Also, it would be decidedly unfair to keep the house rules a secret from the dog, and then get angry and punish the poor critter for inevitably transgressing rules she did not even know existed. Remember: Without adequate education and guidance, the dog will be forced to establish her own rules—doggy rules—and most probably will be at odds with the owner's view of domestic living.

Since most problems develop during the first few days the dog is at home, prospective dog owners must be certain they are quite clear about the principles of housetraining *before* they get a dog. Early misbehaviors quickly become established as the *status quo*—

becoming firmly entrenched as hard-to-break bad habits, which set the precedent for years to come. Make sure to teach your dog good habits right from the start. Good habits are just as hard to break as bad ones!

Ideally, when a new dog comes home, try to arrange for someone to be present as much as possible during the first few days (for adult dogs) or weeks for puppies. With only a little forethought, it is surprisingly easy to find a puppy sitter, such as a retired person, who would be willing to eat from your refrigerator and watch your television while keeping an eye on the newcomer to encourage the dog to play with chew toys and to ensure she goes outside on a regular basis.

POTTY TRAINING

To teach the dog where to relieve herself:

1. never let her make a single mistake;
2. let her know where you want her to go; and
3. handsomely reward her for doing so: "GOOOOOOOD DOG!!!" liver treat, liver treat, liver treat!

Preventing Mistakes

A single mistake is a training disaster, since it heralds many more in future weeks. And each time the dog soils the house, this further reinforces the dog's unfortunate preference for an indoor, carpeted toilet. *Do not let an unhousetrained dog have full run of the house.*

When you are away from home, or cannot pay full attention, confine the dog to an area where elimination is appropriate, such as an outdoor run or, better still, a small, comfortable indoor kennel with access to an outdoor run. When confined in this manner, most dogs will naturally housetrain themselves.

If that's not possible, confine the dog to an area, such as a utility room, kitchen, basement or garage, where elimination may not be desired in the long run but as an interim measure it is certainly preferable to doing it all around the house. Use newspaper to cover the floor of the dog's day room. The newspaper may be used to soak up the urine and to wrap up and dispose of the feces. Once your dog develops a preferred spot for eliminating, it is only necessary to cover that part of the floor with newspaper. The smaller papered area may then be moved (only a little each day) towards the door to the outside. Thus the dog will develop the tendency to go to the door when she needs to relieve herself.

Never confine an unhousetrained dog to a crate for long periods. Doing so would force the dog to soil the crate and ruin its usefulness as an aid for housetraining (see the following discussion).

Teaching Where

In order to teach your dog where you would like her to do her business, you have to be there to direct the proceedings—an obvious, yet often neglected, fact of life. In order to be there to teach the dog *where* to go, you need to know *when* she needs to go. Indeed, the success of housetraining depends on the owner's ability to predict these times. Certainly, a regular feeding schedule will facilitate prediction somewhat, but there is nothing like "loading the deck" and influencing the timing of the outcome yourself!

The first few weeks at home are the most important and influential in your dog's life.

Whenever you are at home, make sure the dog is under constant supervision and/or confined to a small area. If already well trained, simply instruct the dog to lie down in her bed or basket. Alternatively, confine the dog to a crate (doggy den) or tie-down (a short, 18-inch lead that can be clipped to an eye hook in the baseboard near her bed). Short-term close confinement strongly inhibits urination and defecation, since the dog does not want to soil her sleeping area. Thus, when you release the puppydog each hour, she will definitely need to urinate immediately and defecate every third or fourth hour. Keep the dog confined to her doggy den and take her to her intended toilet area each hour, every hour and on the hour.

When taking your dog outside, instruct her to sit quietly before opening the door—she will soon learn to sit by the door when she needs to go out!

Teaching Why

Being able to predict when the dog needs to go enables the owner to be on the spot to praise and reward the dog. Each hour, hurry the dog to the intended toilet area in the yard, issue the appropriate instruction ("Go pee!" or "Go poop!"), then give the dog three to four minutes to produce. Praise and offer a couple of training treats when successful. The treats are important because many people fail to praise their dogs with feeling . . . and housetraining is hardly the time for understatement. So either loosen up and enthusiastically praise that dog: "Wuzzzer-wuzzer-wuzzer, hoooser good wuffer den? Hoooo went pee for Daddy?" Or say "Good dog!" as best you can and offer the treats for effect.

Following elimination is an ideal time for a spot of play-training in the yard or house. Also, an empty dog may be allowed greater freedom around the house for the next half hour or so, just as long as you keep an eye out to make sure she does not get into other kinds of mischief. If you are preoccupied and cannot pay full attention, confine the dog to her doggy den once more to enjoy a peaceful snooze or to play with her many chew toys.

If your dog does not eliminate within the allotted time outside—no biggie! Back to her doggy den, and then try again after another hour.

As I own large dogs, I always feel more relaxed walking an empty dog, knowing that I will not need to finish our stroll weighted down with bags of feces!

Beware of falling into the trap of walking the dog to get her to eliminate. The good ol' dog walk is such an enormous highlight in the dog's life that it represents the single biggest potential reward in domestic dogdom. However, when in a hurry, or during inclement weather, many owners abruptly terminate the walk the moment the dog has done her business. This, in effect, severely punishes the dog for doing the right thing, in the right place at the right time. Consequently, many dogs become strongly inhibited from eliminating outdoors because they know it will signal an abrupt end to an otherwise thoroughly enjoyable walk.

Instead, instruct the dog to relieve herself in the yard prior to going for a walk. If you follow the above instructions, most dogs soon learn to eliminate on cue. As soon as the dog eliminates, praise (and offer a treat or two)—"Good dog! Let's go walkies!" Use the walk as a reward for eliminating in the yard. If the dog does not go, put her back in her doggy den and think about a walk later on. You will find with a "No feces—no walk" policy, your dog will become one of the fastest defecators in the business.

If you do not have a backyard, instruct the dog to eliminate right outside your front door prior to the walk. Not only will this facilitate clean up and disposal of the feces in your own trash can but, also, the walk may again be used as a colossal reward.

CHEWING AND BARKING

Short-term close confinement also teaches the dog that occasional quiet moments are a reality of domestic living. Your puppydog is extremely impressionable during her first few weeks at home. Regular confinement at this time soon exerts a calming influence over the dog's personality. Remember, once the dog is housetrained and calmer, there will be a whole lifetime ahead for the dog to enjoy full run of the house and garden. On the other hand, by letting the newcomer have unrestricted access to the entire household and allowing her to run willy-nilly, she will most certainly develop a bunch of behavior problems in short order, no doubt necessitating confinement later in life. It would not be fair to remedially restrain and confine a dog you have trained, through neglect, to run free.

When confining the dog, make sure she always has an impressive array of suitable chew toys. Kongs and sterilized longbones (both readily available from pet stores) make the best chew toys, since they are hollow and may be stuffed with treats to heighten the dog's interest. For example, by stuffing the little hole at the top of a Kong with a small piece of freeze-dried liver, the dog will not want to leave it alone.

Remember, treats do not have to be junk food and they certainly should not represent extra calories. Rather, treats should be part of each dog's regular daily diet: Some food may be served in the dog's bowl for breakfast and dinner, some food may be used as training treats, and some food may be used for stuffing chew toys. I regularly stuff my dogs' many Kongs with different shaped biscuits and kibble.

Make sure your puppy has suitable chew toys.

The kibble seems to fall out fairly easily, as do the oval-shaped biscuits, thus rewarding the dog instantaneously for checking out the chew toys. The bone-shaped biscuits fall out after a while, rewarding the dog for worrying at the chew toy. But the triangular biscuits never come out. They remain inside the Kong as lures, maintaining the dog's fascination with her chew toy. To further focus the dog's interest, I always make sure to flavor the triangular biscuits by rubbing them with a little cheese or freeze-dried liver.

If stuffed chew toys are reserved especially for times the dog is confined, the puppydog will soon learn to enjoy quiet moments in her doggy den and she will quickly develop a chew-toy habit— a good habit! This is a simple *autoshaping* process; all the owner has to do is set up the situation and the dog all but trains herself— easy and effective. Even when the dog is given run of the house, her first inclination will be to indulge her rewarding chew-toy habit rather than destroy less-attractive household articles, such as curtains, carpets, chairs and compact disks. Similarly, a chew-toy chewer will be less inclined to scratch and chew herself excessively. Also, if the dog busies herself as a recreational chewer, she will be less inclined to develop into a recreational barker or digger when left at home alone.

Stuff a number of chew toys whenever the dog is left confined and remove the extra-special-tasting treats when you return. Your dog will now amuse herself with her chew toys before falling asleep and then resume playing with her chew toys when she expects you to return. Since most owner-absent misbehavior happens right after you leave and right before your expected return, your puppydog will now be conveniently preoccupied with her chew toys at these times.

Come and Sit

Most puppies will happily approach virtually anyone, whether called or not; that is, until they collide with adolescence and

To teach come, call your dog, open your arms as a welcoming signal, wave a toy or a treat and praise for every step in your direction.

develop other more important doggy interests, such as sniffing a multiplicity of exquisite odors on the grass. Your mission, Mr./Ms. Owner, is to teach and reward the pup for coming reliably, willingly and happily when called—and you have just three months to get it done. Unless adequately reinforced, your puppy's tendency to approach people will self-destruct by adolescence.

Call your dog ("Tina, come!"), open your arms (and maybe squat down) as a welcoming signal, waggle a treat or toy as a lure and reward the puppydog when she comes running. Do not wait to praise the dog until she reaches you—she may come 95 percent of the way and then run off after some distraction. Instead, praise the dog's *first* step towards you and continue praising enthusiastically for *every* step she takes in your direction.

When the rapidly approaching puppy dog is three lengths away from impact, instruct her to sit ("Tina, sit!") and hold the lure in front of you in an outstretched hand to prevent her from hitting you mid-chest and knocking you flat on your back! As Tina decelerates to nose the lure, move the treat upwards and backwards just over her muzzle with an upwards motion of your extended arm (palm-upwards). As the dog looks up to follow the lure, she will sit down (if she jumps up, you are holding the lure too high). Praise the dog for sitting. Move backwards and call her again. Repeat this many times over, always praising when Tina comes and sits; on occasion, reward her.

For the first couple of trials, use a training treat both as a lure to entice the dog to come and sit and as a reward for doing so. Thereafter, try to use different items as lures and rewards. For example, lure the dog with a Kong or Frisbee but reward her with a food treat. Or lure the dog with a food treat but pat her and throw a tennis ball as a reward. After just a few repetitions, dispense with the lures and rewards; the dog will begin to respond willingly to your verbal requests and hand signals just for the prospect of praise from your heart and affection from your hands.

Instruct every family member, friend and visitor how to get the dog to come and sit. Invite people over for a series of pooch parties; do not keep the pup a secret—let other people enjoy this puppy, and let the pup enjoy other people. Puppydog parties are not only fun, they easily attract a lot of people to help *you* train *your* dog. Unless you teach your dog how to meet people, that is, to sit for greetings, no doubt the dog will resort to jumping up. Then you and the visitors will get annoyed, and the dog will be punished. This is not fair. *Send out those invitations for puppy parties and teach your dog to be mannerly and socially acceptable.*

Even though your dog quickly masters obedient recalls in the house, her reliability may falter when playing in the backyard or local park. Ironically, it is *the owner* who has unintentionally trained the dog *not* to respond in these instances. By allowing the dog to play and run around and otherwise have a good time, but then to call the dog to put her on leash to take her home, the dog quickly learns playing is fun but training is a drag. Thus, playing in the park becomes a severe distraction, which works against training. Bad news!

Instead, whether playing with the dog off leash or on leash, request her to come at frequent intervals—say, every minute or so. On most occasions, praise and pet the dog for a few seconds while she is sitting, then tell her to go play again. For especially fast recalls, offer a couple of training treats and take the time to praise and pet the dog enthusiastically before releasing her. The dog will learn that coming when called is not necessarily the end of the play session, and neither is it the end of the world; rather, it signals an enjoyable, quality time-out with the owner before resuming play once more. In fact, playing in the park now becomes a very effective life-reward, which works to facilitate training by reinforcing each obedient and timely recall. Good news!

Sit, Down, Stand and Rollover

Teaching the dog a variety of body positions is easy for owner and dog, impressive for spectators and extremely useful for all. Using lure-reward techniques, it is possible to train several positions at once to verbal commands or hand signals (which impress the socks off onlookers).

Sit and ***down***—the two control commands—prevent or resolve nearly a hundred behavior problems. For example, if the dog happily and obediently sits or lies down when requested, she cannot jump on visitors, dash out the front door, run around and chase her tail, pester other dogs, harass cats or annoy family, friends or strangers. Additionally, "Sit" or "Down" are the best emergency commands for off-leash control.

It is easier to teach and maintain a reliable sit than maintain a reliable recall. *Sit* is the purest and simplest of commands—either the dog is sitting or she is not. If there is any change of circumstances or potential danger in the park, for example, simply instruct the dog to sit. If she sits, you have a number of options: Allow the dog to resume playing when she is safe, walk up and put the dog on leash or call the dog. The dog will be much more likely to come when called if she has already acknowledged her compliance by sitting. If the dog does not sit in the park—train her to!

Stand and ***rollover-stay*** are the two positions for examining the dog. Your veterinarian will love you to distraction if you take a little time to teach the dog to stand still and roll over and play possum. Also, your vet bills will be smaller because it will take the veterinarian less time to examine your dog. The rollover-stay is an especially useful command and is really just a variation of the down-stay: Whereas the dog lies prone in the traditional down, she lies supine in the rollover-stay.

As with teaching come and sit, the training techniques to teach the dog to assume all other body positions on cue are user-friendly and dog-friendly. Simply give the appropriate request, lure the dog into the desired body position using a training treat or toy and then *praise* (and maybe reward) the dog as soon as she complies. Try not to touch the dog to get her to respond. If you teach the dog by guiding her into position, the dog will quickly learn that rump-pressure means sit, for example, but as yet you still have no control over your dog if she is just 6 feet away. It will still be necessary to teach the dog to sit on request. So do not make training a time-consuming two-step process; instead, teach the dog to sit to a verbal request or hand signal from the outset. Once the dog sits willingly when requested, by all means use your hands to pet the dog when she does so.

To teach *down* when the dog is already sitting, say "Tina, down!," hold the lure in one hand (palm down) and lower that hand to the floor between the dog's forepaws. As the dog lowers her head to follow the lure, slowly move the lure away from the dog just a fraction (in front of her paws). The dog will lie down as she stretches her nose forward to follow the lure. Praise the dog when she does so. If the dog stands up, you pulled the lure away too far and too quickly.

When teaching the dog to lie down from the standing position, say "Down" and lower the lure to the floor as before. Once the dog has lowered her forequarters and assumed a play bow, gently and slowly move the lure *towards* the dog between her forelegs. Praise the dog as soon as her rear end plops down.

After just a couple of trials it will be possible to alternate sits and downs and have the dog energetically perform doggy push-ups. Praise the dog a lot, and after half a dozen or so push-ups reward the dog with a training treat or toy. You will notice the more energetically you move your arm—upwards (palm up) to get the dog to sit, and downwards (palm down) to get the dog to lie down—the more energetically the dog responds to your requests. Now try training the dog in silence and you will notice she has also learned to respond to hand signals. Yeah! Not too shabby for the first session.

To teach *stand* from the sitting position, say "Tina, stand," slowly move the lure half a dog-length away from the dog's nose, keeping it at nose level, and praise the dog as she stands to follow the lure. As soon

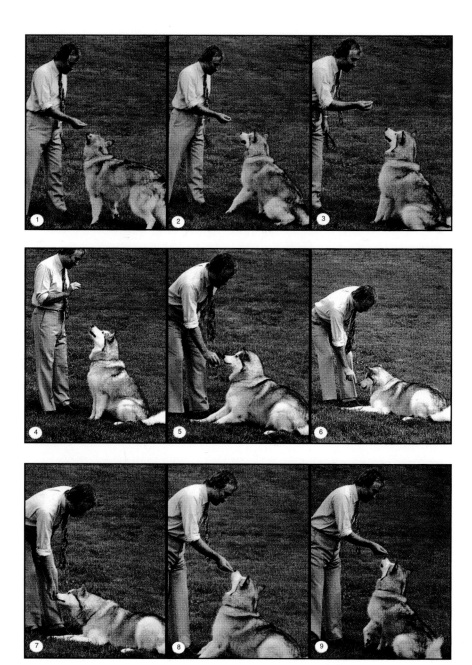

Using a food lure to teach sit, down and stand. 1) "Phoenix, sit." 2) Hand palm upwards, move lure up and back over dog's muzzle. 3) "Good sit, Phoenix!" 4) "Phoenix, down." 5) Hand palm downwards, move lure down to lie between dog's forepaws. 6) "Phoenix, off. Good down, Phoenix!" 7) "Phoenix, sit!" 8) Palm upwards, move lure up and back, keeping it close to dog's muzzle. 9) "Good sit, Phoenix!"

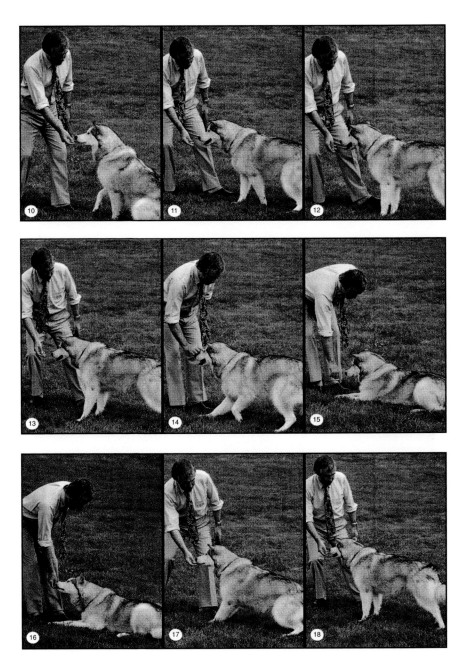

10) "Phoenix, stand!" 11) Move lure away from dog at nose height, then lower it a tad. 12) "Phoenix, off! Good stand, Phoenix!" 13) "Phoenix, down!" 14) Hand palm downwards, move lure down to lie between dog's forepaws. 15) "Phoenix, off! Good down-stay, Phoenix!" 16) "Phoenix, stand!" 17) Move lure away from dog's muzzle up to nose height. 18) "Phoenix, off! Good stand-stay, Phoenix. Now we'll make the vet and groomer happy!"

as the dog stands, lower the lure to just beneath the dog's chin to entice her to look down; otherwise she will stand and then sit immediately. To prompt the dog to stand from the down position, move the lure half a dog-length upwards and away from the dog, holding the lure at standing nose height from the floor.

Teaching **rollover** is best started from the down position, with the dog lying on one side, or at least with both hind legs stretched out on the same side. Say "Tina, bang!" and move the lure backwards and alongside the dog's muzzle to her elbow (on the side of her outstretched hind legs). Once the dog looks to the side and backwards, very slowly move the lure upwards to the dog's shoulder and backbone. Tickling the dog in the goolies (groin area) often invokes a reflex-raising of the hind leg as an appeasement gesture, which facilitates the tendency to roll over. If you move the lure too quickly and the dog jumps into the standing position, have patience and start again. As soon as the dog rolls onto her back, keep the lure stationary and mesmerize the dog with a relaxing tummy rub.

To teach **rollover-stay** when the dog is standing or moving, say "Tina, bang!" and give the appropriate hand signal (with index finger pointed and thumb cocked in true Sam Spade fashion), then in one fluid movement lure her to first lie down and then rollover-stay as above.

Teaching the dog to **stay** in each of the above four positions becomes a piece of cake after first teaching the dog not to worry at the toy or treat training lure. This is best accomplished by hand feeding dinner kibble. Hold a piece of kibble firmly in your hand and softly instruct "Off!" Ignore any licking and slobbering *for however long the dog worries at the treat,* but say "Take it!" and offer the kibble *the instant* the dog breaks contact with her muzzle. Repeat this a few times, and then up the ante and insist the dog remove her muzzle for one whole second before offering the kibble. Then progressively refine your criteria and have the dog not touch your hand (or treat) for longer and longer periods on each trial, such as for two seconds, four seconds, then six, ten, fifteen, twenty, thirty seconds and so on.

The dog soon learns: (1) worrying at the treat never gets results, whereas (2) noncontact is often rewarded after a variable time lapse.

Teaching *"Off!"* has many useful applications in its own right. Additionally, instructing the dog not to touch a training lure often produces spontaneous and magical stays. Request the dog to stand-stay, for example, and not to touch the lure. At first set your sights on a short two-second stay before rewarding the dog. (Remember, every long journey begins with a single step.) However, on subsequent trials, gradually and progressively increase the length of stay required to receive a reward. In no time at all your dog will stand calmly for a minute or so.

Relevancy Training

Once you have taught the dog what you expect her to do when requested to come, sit, lie down, stand, roll-over and stay, the time is right to teach the dog *why* she should comply with your wishes. The secret is to have many (*many*) extremely short training interludes (two to five seconds each) at numerous (*numerous*) times during the course of the dog's day. Especially work with the dog immediately *before* the dog's good times and *during* the dog's good times. For example, ask your dog to sit and/or lie down each time before opening doors, serving meals, offering treats and tummy rubs; ask the dog to perform a few controlled doggy push-ups before letting her off leash or throwing a tennis ball; and perhaps request the dog to sit-down-sit-stand-down-stand-rollover before inviting her to cuddle on the couch.

Similarly, request the dog to sit many times during play or on walks, and in no time at all the dog will be only too pleased to follow your instructions because she has learned that a compliant response heralds all sorts of goodies. Basically all you are trying to teach the dog is how to say please: "Please throw the tennis ball. Please may I snuggle on the couch."

Remember, it is important to keep training interludes short and to have many short sessions each and every day. The shortest (and most useful) session comprises asking the dog to sit and then go play during a play session. When trained this way, your dog will soon associate training with good times. In fact, the dog may be unable to distinguish between training and good times and, indeed, there should be no distinction. The warped concept that training involves forcing the dog to comply and/or dominating her will is totally at odds with the picture of a truly well-trained dog. In reality, enjoying a game of training with a dog is no different from enjoying a game of backgammon or tennis with a friend; and walking with a dog should be no different from strolling with a spouse, or with buddies on the golf course.

Walk by Your Side

Many people attempt to teach a dog to heel by putting her on a leash and physically correcting the dog when she makes mistakes. There are a number of things seriously wrong with this approach, the first being that most people do not want precision heeling; rather, they simply want the dog to follow or walk by their side. Second, when physically restrained during "training," even though the dog may grudgingly mope by your side when "handcuffed" on leash, let's see what happens when she is off leash. History! The dog is in the next county because she never enjoyed walking with you on leash and you have no control over her off leash. So let's just teach the dog off leash from the outset to *want* to walk with us. Third, if the dog has not been trained to heel, it is a trifle hasty to think about punishing the poor dog for making mistakes and breaking heeling rules she didn't even know existed. This is simply not fair! Surely, if the dog had been adequately taught how to heel, she would seldom make mistakes and hence there would be no need to correct the dog. Remember, each mistake and each correction (punishment) advertise the trainer's inadequacy, not the dog's. The dog is not stubborn, she is not stupid and she is not bad. Even if she were, she would still require training, so let's train her properly.

Let's teach the dog to *enjoy* following us and to *want* to walk by our side off leash. Then it will be easier to teach high-precision off-leash heeling patterns if desired. Before going on outdoor walks, it is necessary to teach the dog not to pull. Then it becomes easy to teach on-leash walking and heeling because the dog already wants to walk with you, she is familiar with the desired walking and heeling positions and she knows not to pull.

FOLLOWING

Start by training your dog to follow you. Many puppies will follow if you simply walk away from them and maybe click your fingers or chuckle. Adult dogs may require additional enticement to stimulate them to follow, such as a training lure or, at the very least, a lively trainer. To teach the dog to follow: (1) keep walking and (2) walk away from the dog. If the dog attempts to lead or lag, change pace; slow down if the dog forges too far ahead, but speed up if she lags too far behind. Say "Steady!" or "Easy!" each time before you slow down and "Quickly!" or "Hustle!" each time before you speed up, and the dog will learn to change pace on cue. If the dog lags or leads too far, or if she wanders right or left, simply walk quickly in the opposite direction and maybe even run away from the dog and hide.

Practicing is a lot of fun; you can set up a course in your home, yard or park to do this. Indoors, entice the dog to follow upstairs, into a bedroom, into the bathroom, downstairs, around the living room couch, zigzagging between dining room chairs and into the kitchen for dinner. Outdoors, get the dog to follow around park benches, trees, shrubs and along walkways and lines in the grass. (For safety outdoors, it is advisable to attach a long line on the dog, but never exert corrective tension on the line.)

Remember, following has a lot to do with attitude—
your attitude! Most probably your dog will *not* want to
follow Mr. Grumpy Troll with the personality of wilted
lettuce. Lighten up—walk with a jaunty step, whistle a
happy tune, sing, skip and tell jokes to your dog and
she will be right there by your side.

BY YOUR SIDE

It is smart to train the dog to walk close on one side or
the other—either side will do, your choice. When walking, jogging or cycling, it is generally bad news to have
the dog suddenly cut in front of you. In fact, I train my
dogs to walk "By my side" and "Other side"—both very
useful instructions. It is possible to position the dog
fairly accurately by looking to the appropriate side and
clicking your fingers or slapping your thigh on that
side. A precise positioning may be attained by holding
a training lure, such as a chew toy, tennis ball or food
treat. Stop and stand still several times throughout the
walk, just as you would when window shopping or
meeting a friend. Use the lure to make sure the dog
slows down and stays close whenever you stop.

When teaching the dog to heel, we generally want
her to sit in heel position when we stop. Teach heel

Using a toy to teach sit-heel-sit sequences: 1) "Phoenix, sit!" Standing still, move lure up and back over dog's muzzle . . . 2) to position dog sitting in heel position on your left side. 3) Say "Phoenix, heel!" and walk ahead, wagging lure in left hand. Change lure to right hand in preparation for sit signal. Say "Sit" and then . . .

position at the standstill and the dog will learn that the default heel position is sitting by your side (left or right—your choice, unless you wish to compete in obedience trials, in which case the dog must heel on the left).

Several times a day, stand up and call your dog to come and sit in heel position—"Tina, heel!" For example, instruct the dog to come to heel each time there are commercials on TV, or each time you turn a page of a novel, and the dog will get it in a single evening.

Practice straight-line heeling and turns separately. With the dog sitting at heel, teach her to turn in place. After each quarter-turn, half-turn or full turn in place, lure the dog to sit at heel. Now it's time for short straight-line heeling sequences, no more than a few steps at a time. Always think of heeling in terms of sit-heel-sit sequences—start and end with the dog in position and do your best to keep her there when moving. Progressively increase the number of steps in each sequence. When the dog remains close for 20 yards of straight-line heeling, it is time to add a few turns and then sign up for a happy-heeling obedience class to get some advice from the experts.

4) use hand signal to lure dog to sit as you stop. Eventually, dog will sit automatically at heel whenever you stop. 5) "Good dog!"

No Pulling on Leash

You can start teaching your dog not to pull on leash anywhere—in front of the television or outdoors—but regardless of location, you must not take a single step with tension in the leash. For a reason known only to dogs, even just a couple of paces of pulling on leash is intrinsically motivating and diabolically rewarding. Instead, attach the leash to the dog's collar, grasp the other end firmly with both hands held close to your chest, and stand still—do not budge an inch. Have somebody watch you with a stopwatch to time your progress, or else you will never believe this will work and so you will not even try the exercise, and your shoulder and the dog's neck will be traumatized for years to come.

Stand still and wait for the dog to stop pulling, and to sit and/or lie down. All dogs stop pulling and sit eventually. Most take only a couple of minutes; the all-time record is 22½ minutes. Time how long it takes. Gently praise the dog when she stops pulling, and as soon as she sits, enthusiastically praise the dog and take just one step forward, then immediately stand still. This single step usually demonstrates the ballistic reinforcing nature of pulling on leash; most dogs explode to the end of the leash, so be prepared for the strain. Stand firm and wait for the dog to sit again. Repeat this half a dozen times and you will probably notice a progressive reduction in the force of the dog's one-step explosions and a radical reduction in the time it takes for the dog to sit each time.

As the dog learns "Sit we go" and "Pull we stop," she will begin to walk forward calmly with each single step and automatically sit when you stop. Now try two steps before you stop. Wooooooo! Scary! When the dog has mastered two steps at a time, try for three. After each success, progressively increase the number of steps in the sequence: try four steps and then six, eight, ten and twenty steps before stopping. Congratulations! You are now walking the dog on leash.

Whenever walking with the dog (off leash or on leash), make sure you stop periodically to practice a few position commands and stays before instructing the dog to "Walk on!" (Remember, you want the dog to be compliant everywhere, not just in the kitchen when her dinner is at hand.) For example, stopping every 25 yards to briefly train the dog amounts to over 200 training interludes within a single 3-mile stroll. And each training session is in a different location. You will not believe the improvement within just the first mile of the first walk.

To put it another way, integrating training into a walk offers 200 separate opportunities to use the continuance of the walk as a reward to reinforce the dog's education. Moreover, some training interludes may comprise continuing education for the dog's walking skills: Alternate short periods of the dog walking calmly by your side with periods when the dog is allowed to sniff and investigate the environment. Now sniffing odors on the grass and meeting other dogs become rewards which reinforce the dog's calm and mannerly demeanor. Good Lord! Whatever next? Many enjoyable walks together of course. Happy trails!

THE IMPORTANCE OF TRICKS

Nothing will improve a dog's quality of life better than having a few tricks under her belt. Teaching any trick expands the dog's vocabulary, which facilitates communication and improves the owner's control. Also, specific tricks help prevent and resolve specific behavior problems. For example, by teaching the dog to fetch her toys, the dog learns carrying a toy makes the owner happy and, therefore, will be more likely to chew her toy than other inappropriate items.

More important, teaching tricks prompts owners to lighten up and train with a sunny disposition. Really, tricks should be no different from any other behaviors we put on cue. But they are. When teaching tricks, owners have a much sweeter attitude, which in turn motivates the dog and improves her willingness to comply. The dog feels tricks are a blast, but formal commands are a drag. In fact, tricks are so enjoyable, they may be used as rewards in training by asking the dog to come, sit and down-stay and then rollover for a tummy rub. Go on, try it: Crack a smile and even giggle when the dog promptly and willingly lies down and stays.

Most important, performing tricks prompts onlookers to smile and giggle. Many people are scared of dogs, especially large ones. And nothing can be more off-putting for a dog than to be constantly confronted by strangers who don't like her because of her size or the way she looks. Uneasy people put the dog on edge, causing her to back off and bark, only frightening people all the more. And so a vicious circle develops, with the people's fear fueling the dog's fear *and vice versa*. Instead, tie a pink ribbon to your dog's collar and practice all sorts of tricks on walks and in the park, and you will be pleasantly amazed how it changes people's attitudes toward your friendly dog. The dog's repertoire of tricks is limited only by the trainer's imagination. Below I have described three of my favorites:

SPEAK AND SHUSH

The training sequence involved in teaching a dog to bark on request is no different from that used when training any behavior on cue: request—lure—response—reward. As always, the secret of success lies in finding an effective lure. If the dog always barks at the doorbell, for example, say "Rover, speak!", have an accomplice ring the doorbell, then reward the dog for barking. After a few woofs, ask Rover to "Shush!", waggle a food treat under her nose (to entice her to sniff and thus to shush), praise her when quiet and eventually offer the treat as a reward. Alternate "Speak" and "Shush," progressively increasing the length of shush-time between each barking bout.

PLAY BOW

With the dog standing, say "Bow!" and lower the food lure (palm upwards) to rest between the dog's forepaws. Praise as the dog lowers her forequarters and sternum to the ground (as when teaching the down), but then lure the dog to stand and offer the treat. On successive trials, gradually increase the length of time the dog is required to remain in the play bow posture in order to gain a food reward. If the dog's rear end collapses into a down, say nothing and offer no reward; simply start over.

BE A BEAR

With the dog sitting backed into a corner to prevent her from toppling over backwards, say "Be a bear!" With bent paw and palm down, raise a lure upwards and backwards along the top of the dog's muzzle. Praise the dog when she sits up on her haunches and offer the treat as a reward. To prevent the dog from standing on her hind legs, keep the lure closer to the dog's muzzle. On each trial, progressively increase the length of time the dog is required to sit up to receive a food reward. Since lure-reward training is so easy, teach the dog to stand and walk on her hind legs as well!

Teaching "Be a Bear"

127

chapter 9

Getting
Active
with your Dog

by Bardi McLennan

Once you and your dog have graduated from basic obedience training and are beginning to work together as a team, you can take part in the growing world of dog activities. There are so many fun things to do with your dog! Just remember, people and dogs don't always learn at the same pace, so don't be upset if you (or your dog) need more than two basic training courses before your team becomes operational. Even smart dogs don't go straight to college from kindergarten!

Just as there are events geared to certain types of dogs, so there are ones that are more appealing to certain types of people. In some activities, you give the commands and your dog does the work (upland game hunting is one example), while in others, such as agility, you'll both get a workout. You may want to aim for prestigious titles to add to your dog's name, or you may want nothing more than the sheer enjoyment of being around other people and their dogs. Passive or active, participation has its own rewards.

Consider your dog's physical capabilities when looking into any of the canine activities. It's easy to see that a Basset Hound is not built for the racetrack, nor would a Chihuahua be the breed of choice for pulling a sled. A loyal dog will attempt almost anything you ask him to do, so it is up to you to know your

All dogs seem to love playing flyball.

dog's limitations. A dog must be physically sound in order to compete at any level in athletic activities, and being mentally sound is a definite plus. Advanced age, however, may not be a deterrent. Many dogs still hunt and herd at ten or twelve years of age. It's entirely possible for dogs to be "fit at 50." Take your dog for a checkup, explain to your vet the type of activity you have in mind and be guided by his or her findings.

You needn't be restricted to breed-specific sports if it's only fun you're after. Certain AKC activities are limited to designated breeds; however, as each new trial, test or sport has grown in popularity, so has the variety of breeds encouraged to participate at a fun level.

But don't shortchange your fun, or that of your dog, by thinking only of the basic function of her breed. Once a dog has learned how to learn, she can be taught to do just about anything as long as the size of the dog is right for the job and you both think it is fun and rewarding. In other words, you are a team.

To get involved in any of the activities detailed in this chapter, look for the names and addresses of the organizations that sponsor them in Chapter 13. You can also ask your breeder or a local dog trainer for contacts.

You can compete in obedience trials with a well trained dog.

Official American Kennel Club Activities

The following tests and trials are some of the events sanctioned by the AKC and sponsored by various dog clubs. Your dog's expertise will be rewarded with impressive titles. You can participate just for fun, or be competitive and go for those awards.

OBEDIENCE

Training classes begin with pups as young as three months of age in kindergarten puppy training, then advance to pre-novice (all exercises on lead) and go on to novice, which is where you'll start off-lead work. In obedience classes dogs learn to sit, stay, heel and come through a variety of exercises. Once you've got the basics down, you can enter obedience trials and work toward earning your dog's first degree, a C.D. (Companion Dog).

The next level is called "Open," in which jumps and retrieves perk up the dog's interest. Passing grades in competition at this level earn a C.D.X. (Companion Dog Excellent). Beyond that lies the goal of the most ambitious—Utility (U.D. and even U.D.X. or OTCh, an Obedience Champion).

AGILITY

All dogs can participate in the latest canine sport to have gained worldwide popularity for its fun and excitement, agility. It began in England as a canine version of horse show-jumping, but because dogs are more agile and able to perform on verbal commands, extra feats were added such as climbing, balancing and racing through tunnels or in and out of weave poles. Many of the obstacles (regulation or homemade) can be set up in your own backyard. If the agility bug bites, you could end up in international competition!

For starters, your dog should be obedience trained, even though, in the beginning, the lessons may all be taught on lead. Once the dog understands the commands (and you do, too), it's as easy as guiding the dog over a prescribed course, one obstacle at a time. In competition, the race is against the clock, so wear your running shoes! The dog starts with 200 points and the judge deducts for infractions and misadventures along the way.

All dogs seem to love agility and respond to it as if they were being turned loose in a playground paradise. Your dog's enthusiasm will be contagious; agility turns into great fun for dog and owner.

FIELD TRIALS AND HUNTING TESTS

There are field trials and hunting tests for the sporting breeds—retrievers, spaniels and pointing breeds, and for some hounds—Bassets, Beagles and Dachshunds. Field trials are competitive events that test a dog's ability to perform the functions for which she was bred. Hunting tests, which are open to retrievers,

TITLES AWARDED BY THE AKC

Conformation: Ch. (Champion)

Obedience: CD (Companion Dog); CDX (Companion Dog Excellent); UD (Utility Dog); UDX (Utility Dog Excellent); OTCh. (Obedience Trial Champion)

Field: JH (Junior Hunter); SH (Senior Hunter); MH (Master Hunter); AFCh. (Amateur Field Champion); FCh. (Field Champion)

Lure Coursing: JC (Junior Courser); SC (Senior Courser)

Herding: HT (Herding Tested); PT (Pre-Trial Tested); HS (Herding Started); HI (Herding Intermediate); HX (Herding Excellent); HCh. (Herding Champion)

Tracking: TD (Tracking Dog); TDX (Tracking Dog Excellent)

Agility: NAD (Novice Agility); OAD (Open Agility); ADX (Agility Excellent); MAX (Master Agility)

Earthdog Tests: JE (Junior Earthdog); SE (Senior Earthdog); ME (Master Earthdog)

Canine Good Citizen: CGC

Combination: DC (Dual Champion—Ch. and Fch.); TC (Triple Champion—Ch., Fch., and OTCh.)

spaniels and pointing breeds only, are noncompetitive and are a means of judging the dog's ability as well as that of the handler.

Hunting is a very large and complex part of canine sports, and if you own one of the breeds that hunts, the events are a great treat for your dog and you. He gets to do what he was bred for, and you get to work with him and watch him do it. You'll be proud of and amazed at what your dog can do.

Retrievers and other sporting breeds get to do what they're bred to in hunting tests.

Fortunately, the AKC publishes a series of booklets on these events, which outline the rules and regulations and include a glossary of the sometimes complicated terms. The AKC also publishes newsletters for field trialers and hunting test enthusiasts. The United Kennel Club (UKC) also has informative materials for the hunter and his dog.

HERDING TESTS AND TRIALS

Herding, like hunting, dates back to the first known uses man made of dogs. The interest in herding today is widespread, and if you own a herding breed, you can join in the activity. Herding dogs are tested for their natural skills to keep a flock of ducks, sheep or cattle together. If your dog shows potential, you can start at the testing level, where your dog can earn a title for showing an inherent herding ability. With training you can advance to the trial level, where your dog should be capable of controlling even difficult livestock in diverse situations.

LURE COURSING

The AKC Tests and Trials for Lure Coursing are open to traditional sighthounds—Greyhounds, Whippets,

Borzoi, Salukis, Afghan Hounds, Ibizan Hounds and Scottish Deerhounds—as well as to Basenjis and Rhodesian Ridgebacks. Hounds are judged on overall ability, follow, speed, agility and endurance. This is possibly the most exciting of the trials for spectators, because the speed and agility of the dogs is awesome to watch as they chase the lure (or "course") in heats of two or three dogs at a time.

TRACKING

Tracking is another activity in which almost any dog can compete because every dog that sniffs the ground when taken outdoors is, in fact, tracking. The hard part comes when the rules as to what, when and where the dog tracks are determined by a person, not the dog! Tracking tests cover a large area of fields, woods and roads. The tracks are laid hours before the dogs go to work on them, and include "tricks" like cross-tracks and sharp turns. If you're interested in search-and-rescue work, this is the place to start.

This tracking dog is hot on the trail.

EARTHDOG TESTS FOR SMALL TERRIERS AND DACHSHUNDS

These tests are open to Australian, Bedlington, Border, Cairn, Dandie Dinmont, Smooth and Wire Fox, Lakeland, Norfolk, Norwich, Scottish, Sealyham, Skye, Welsh and West Highland White Terriers as well as Dachshunds. The dogs need no prior training for this terrier sport. There is a qualifying test on the day of the event, so dog and handler learn the rules on the spot. These tests, or "digs," sometimes end with informal races in the late afternoon.

Here are some of the extracurricular obedience and racing activities that are not regulated by the AKC or UKC, but are generally run by clubs or a group of dog fanciers and are often open to all.

Canine Freestyle This activity is something new on the scene and is variously likened to dancing, dressage or ice skating. It is meant to show the athleticism of the dog, but also requires showmanship on the part of the dog's handler. If you and your dog like to ham it up for friends, you might want to look into freestyle.

Lure coursing lets sighthounds do what they do best—run!

Scent Hurdle Racing Scent hurdle racing is purely a fun activity sponsored by obedience clubs with members forming competing teams. The height of the hurdles is based on the size of the shortest dog on the team. On a signal, one team dog is released on each of two side-by-side courses and must clear every hurdle before picking up its own dumbbell from a platform and returning over the jumps to the handler. As each dog returns, the next on that team is sent. Of course, that is what the dogs are supposed to do. When the dogs improvise (going under or around the hurdles, stealing another dog's dumbbell, and so forth), it no doubt frustrates the handlers, but just adds to the fun for everyone else.

Flyball This type of racing is similar, but after negotiating the four hurdles, the dog comes to a flyball box, steps on a lever that releases a tennis ball into the air, catches the ball and returns over the hurdles to the starting point. This game also becomes extremely fun for spectators because the dogs sometimes cheat by catching a ball released by the dog in the next lane. Three titles can be earned—Flyball Dog (F.D.), Flyball Dog Excellent (F.D.X.) and Flyball Dog Champion (Fb.D.Ch.)—all awarded by the North American Flyball Association, Inc.

Dogsledding The name conjures up the Rocky Mountains or the frigid North, but you can find dogsled clubs in such unlikely spots as Maryland, North Carolina and Virginia! Dogsledding is primarily for the Nordic breeds such as the Alaskan Malamutes, Siberian Huskies and Samoyeds, but other breeds can try. There are some practical backyard applications to this sport, too. With parental supervision, almost any strong dog could pull a child's sled.

Coming over the A-frame on an agility course.

These are just some of the many recreational ways you can get to know and understand your multifaceted dog better and have fun doing it.

chapter 10

Your Dog
and your
Family

by Bardi McLennan

Adding a dog automatically increases your family by one, no matter whether you live alone in an apartment or are part of a mother, father and six kids household. The single-person family is fair game for numerous and varied canine misconceptions as to who is dog and who pays the bills, whereas a dog in a houseful of children will consider himself to be just one of the gang, littermates all. One dog and one child may give a dog reason to believe they are both kids or both dogs.

Either interpretation requires parental supervision and sometimes speedy intervention.

As soon as one paw goes through the door into your home, Rufus (or Rufina) has to make many adjustments to become a part of your family. Your job is to make him fit in as painlessly as possible. An older dog may have some frame of reference from past experience, but to a 10-week-old puppy, everything is brand new: people, furniture, stairs, when and where people eat, sleep or watch TV, his own place and everyone else's space, smells, sounds, outdoors—everything!

Puppies, and newly acquired dogs of any age, do not need what we think of as "freedom." If you leave a new dog or puppy loose in the house, you will almost certainly return to chaotic destruction and the dog will forever after equate your homecoming with a time of punishment to be dreaded. It is unfair to give your dog what amounts to "freedom to get into trouble." Instead, confine him to a crate for brief periods of your absence (up to three or four hours) and, for the long haul, a workday for example, confine him to one untrashable area with his own toys, a bowl of water and a radio left on (low) in another room.

Lots of pets get along with each other just fine.

For the first few days, when not confined, put Rufus on a long leash tied to your wrist or waist. This umbilical cord method enables the dog to learn all about you from your body language and voice, and to learn by his own actions which things in the house are NO! and which ones are rewarded by "Good dog." House-training will be easier with the pup always by your side. Speaking of which, accidents do happen. That goal of "completely housetrained" takes up to a year, or the length of time it takes the pup to mature.

The All-Adult Family

Most dogs in an adults-only household today are likely to be latchkey pets, with no one home all day but the dog. When you return after a tough day on the job, the dog can and should be your relaxation therapy. But going home can instead be a daily frustration.

Separation anxiety is a very common problem for the dog in a working household. It may begin with whines and barks of loneliness, but it will soon escalate into a frenzied destruction derby. That is why it is so important to set aside the time to teach a dog to relax when left alone in his confined area and to understand that he can trust you to return.

Let the dog get used to your work schedule in easy stages. Confine him to one room and go in and out of that room over and over again. Be casual about it. No physical, voice or eye contact. When the pup no longer even notices your comings and goings, leave the house for varying lengths of time, returning to stay home for a few minutes and gradually increasing the time away. This training can take days, but the dog is learning that you haven't left him forever and that he can trust you.

Any time you leave the dog, but especially during this training period, be casual about your departure. No anxiety-building fond farewells. Just "Bye" and go! Remember the "Good dog" when you return to find everything more or less as you left it.

If things are a mess (or even a disaster) when you return, greet the dog, take him outside to eliminate, and then put him in his crate while you clean up. Rant and rave in the shower! *Do not* punish the dog. You were not there when it happened, and the rule is: Only punish as you catch the dog in the act of wrongdoing. Obviously, it makes sense to get your latchkey puppy when you'll have a week or two to spend on these training essentials.

Family weekend activities should include Rufus whenever possible. Depending on the pup's age, now is the time for a long walk in the park, playtime in the backyard, a hike in the woods. Socializing is as important as health care, good food and physical exercise, so visiting Aunt Emma or Uncle Harry and the next-door neighbor's dog or cat is essential to developing an outgoing, friendly temperament in your pet.

If you are a single adult, socializing Rufus at home and away will prevent him from becoming overly protective of you (or just overly attached) and will also prevent such behavioral problems as dominance or fear of strangers.

Babies

Whether already here or on the way, babies figure larger than life in the eyes of a dog. If the dog is there first, let him in on all your baby preparations in the house. When baby arrives, let Rufus sniff any item of clothing that has been on the baby before Junior comes home. Then let Mom greet the dog first before introducing the new family member. Hold the baby down for the dog to see and sniff, but make sure someone's holding the dog on lead in case of any sudden moves. Don't play keep-away or tease the dog with the baby, which only invites undesirable jumping up.

The dog and the baby are "family," and for starters can be treated almost as equals. Things rapidly change, however, especially when baby takes to creeping around on all fours on the dog's turf or, better yet, has yummy pudding all over her face and hands! That's when a lot of things in the dog's and baby's lives become more separate than equal.

Dogs are perfect confidants.

Toddlers make terrible dog owners, but if you can't avoid the combination, use patient discipline (that is, positive teaching rather than punishment), and use time-outs before you run out of patience.

139

A dog and a baby (or toddler, or an assertive young child) should never be left alone together. Take the dog with you or confine him. With a baby or youngsters in the house, you'll have plenty of use for that wonderful canine safety device called a crate!

Young Children

Any dog in a house with kids will behave pretty much as the kids do, good or bad. But even good dogs and good children can get into trouble when play becomes rowdy and active.

Teach children how to play nicely with a puppy.

Legs bobbing up and down, shrill voices screeching, a ball hurtling overhead, all add up to exuberant frustration for a dog who's just trying to be part of the gang. In a pack of puppies, any legs or toys being chased would be caught by a set of teeth, and all the pups involved would understand that is how the game is played. Kids do not understand this, nor do parents tolerate it. Bring Rufus indoors before you have reason to regret it. This is time-out, not a punishment.

You can explain the situation to the children and tell them they must play quieter games until the puppy learns not to grab them with his mouth. Unfortunately, you can't explain it that easily to the dog. With adult supervision, they will learn how to play together.

Young children love to tease. Sticking their faces or wiggling their hands or fingers in the dog's face is teasing. To another person it might be just annoying, but it is threatening to a dog. There's another difference: We can make the child stop by an explanation, but the only way a dog can stop it is with a warning growl and then with teeth. Teasing is the major cause of children being bitten by their pets. Treat it seriously.

Older Children

The best age for a child to get a first dog is between the ages of 8 and 12. That's when kids are able to accept some real responsibility for their pet. Even so, take the child's vow of "I will never *ever* forget to feed (brush, walk, etc.) the dog" for what it's worth: a child's good intention at that moment. Most kids today have extra lessons, soccer practice, Little League, ballet, and so forth piled on top of school schedules. There will be many times when Mom will have to come to the dog's rescue. "I walked the dog for you so you can set the table for me" is one way to get around a missed appointment without laying on blame or guilt.

Kids in this age group make excellent obedience trainers because they are into the teaching/learning process themselves and they lack the self-consciousness of adults. Attending a dog show is something the whole family can enjoy, and watching Junior Showmanship may catch the eye of the kids. Older children can begin to get involved in many of the recreational activities that were reviewed in the previous chapter. Some of the agility obstacles, for example, can be set up in the backyard as a family project (with an adult making sure all the equipment is safe and secure for the dog).

Older kids are also beginning to look to the future, and may envision themselves as veterinarians or trainers or show dog handlers or writers of the next Lassie best-seller. Dogs are perfect confidants for these dreams. They won't tell a soul.

Other Pets

Introduce all pets tactfully. In a dog/cat situation, hold the dog, not the cat. Let two dogs meet on neutral turf—a stroll in the park or a walk down the street—with both on loose leads to permit all the normal canine ways of saying hello, including routine sniffing, circling, more sniffing, and so on. Small creatures such as hamsters, chinchillas or mice must be kept safe from their natural predators (dogs and cats).

Festive Family Occasions

Parties are great for people, but not necessarily for puppies. Until all the guests have arrived, put the dog in his crate or in a room where he won't be disturbed. A socialized dog can join the fun later as long as he's not underfoot, annoying guests or into the hors d'oeuvres.

There are a few dangers to consider, too. Doors opening and closing can allow a puppy to slip out unnoticed in the confusion, and you'll be organizing a search party instead of playing host or hostess. Party food and buffet service are not for dogs. Let Rufus party in his crate with a nice big dog biscuit.

At Christmas time, not only are tree decorations dangerous and breakable (and perhaps family heirlooms), but extreme caution should be taken with the lights, cords and outlets for the tree lights and any other festive lighting. Occasionally a dog lifts a leg, ignoring the fact that the tree is indoors. To avoid this, use a canine repellent, made for gardens, on the tree. Or keep him out of the tree room unless supervised. And whatever you do, *don't* invite trouble by hanging his toys on the tree!

Car Travel

Before you plan a vacation by car or RV with Rufus, be sure he enjoys car travel. Nothing spoils a holiday quicker than a carsick dog! Work within the dog's comfort level. Get in the car with the dog in his crate or attached to a canine car safety belt and just sit there until he relaxes. That's all. Next time, get in the car, turn on the engine and go nowhere. Just sit. When that is okay, turn on the engine and go around the block. Now you can go for a ride and include a stop where you get out, leaving the dog for a minute or two.

On a warm day, always park in the shade and leave windows open several inches. And return quickly. It only takes 10 minutes for a car to become an overheated steel death trap.

Motel or Pet Motel?

Not all motels or hotels accept pets, but you have a much better choice today than even a few years ago. To find a dog-friendly lodging, look at *On the Road Again With Man's Best Friend*, a series of directories that detail bed and breakfasts, inns, family resorts and other hotels/motels. Some places require a refundable deposit to cover any damage incurred by the dog. More B&Bs accept pets now, but some restrict the size.

If taking Rufus with you is not feasible, check out boarding kennels in your area. Your veterinarian may offer this service, or recommend a kennel or two he or she is familiar with. Go see the facilities for yourself, ask about exercise, diet, housing, and so on. Or, if you'd rather have Rufus stay home, look into bonded petsitters, many of whom will also bring in the mail and water your plants.

chapter 11

Your Dog
and your
Community

by Bardi McLennan

Step outside your home with your dog and you are no longer just family, you are both part of your community. This is when the phrase "responsible pet ownership" takes on serious implications. For starters, it means you pick up after your dog—not just occasionally, but every time your dog eliminates away from home. That means you have joined the Plastic Baggy Brigade! You always have plastic sandwich bags in your pocket and several in the car. It means you teach your kids how to use them, too. If you think this is "yucky," just imagine what

the person (a non-doggy person) who inadvertently steps in the mess thinks!

Your responsibility extends to your neighbors: To their ears (no annoying barking); to their property (their garbage, their lawn, their flower beds, their cat—especially their cat); to their kids (on bikes, at play); to their kids' toys and sports equipment.

There are numerous dog-related laws, ranging from simple dog licensing and leash laws to those holding you liable for any physical injury or property damage done by your dog. These laws are in place to protect everyone in the community, including you and your dog. There are town ordinances and state laws which are by no means the same in all towns or all states. Ignorance of the law won't get you off the hook. The time to find out what the laws are where you live is now.

Be sure your dog's license is current. This is not just a good local ordinance, it can make the difference between finding your lost dog or not.

Many states now require proof of rabies vaccination and that the dog has been spayed or neutered before issuing a license. At the same time, keep up the dog's annual immunizations.

Dressing your dog up makes him appealing to strangers.

Never let your dog run loose in the neighborhood. This will not only keep you on the right side of the leash law, it's the outdoor version of the rule about not giving your dog "freedom to get into trouble."

Good Canine Citizen

Sometimes it's hard for a dog's owner to assess whether or not the dog is sufficiently socialized to be accepted by the community at large. Does Rufus or Rufina display good, controlled behavior in public? The AKC's Canine Good Citizen program is available through many dog organizations. If your dog passes the test, the title "CGC" is earned.

The overall purpose is to turn your dog into a good neighbor and to teach you about your responsibility to your community as a dog owner. Here are the ten things your dog must do willingly:

1. Accept a stranger stopping to chat with you.
2. Sit and be petted by a stranger.
3. Allow a stranger to handle him or her as a groomer or veterinarian would.
4. Walk nicely on a loose lead.
5. Walk calmly through a crowd.
6. Sit and down on command, then stay in a sit or down position while you walk away.
7. Come when called.
8. Casually greet another dog.
9. React confidently to distractions.
10. Accept being left alone with someone other than you and not become overly agitated or nervous.

Schools and Dogs

Schools are getting involved with pet ownership on an educational level. It has been proven that children who are kind to animals are humane in their attitude toward other people as adults.

A dog is a child's best friend, and so children are often primary pet owners, if not the primary caregivers. Unfortunately, they are also the ones most often bitten by dogs. This occurs due to a lack of understanding that pets, no matter how sweet, cuddly and loving, are still animals. Schools, along with parents, dog clubs, dog fanciers and the AKC, are working to change all that with video programs for children not only in grade school, but in the nursery school and pre-kindergarten age group. Teaching youngsters how to be responsible dog owners is important community work. When your dog has a CGC, volunteer to take part in an educational classroom event put on by your dog club.

Boy Scout Merit Badge

A Merit Badge for Dog Care can be earned by any Boy Scout ages 11 to 18. The requirements are not easy, but amount to a complete course in responsible dog care and general ownership. Here are just a few of the things a Scout must do to earn that badge:

> Point out ten parts of the dog using the correct names.

> Give a report (signed by parent or guardian) on your care of the dog (feeding, food used, housing, exercising, grooming and bathing), plus what has been done to keep the dog healthy.

> Explain the right way to obedience train a dog, and demonstrate three comments.

> Several of the requirements have to do with health care, including first aid, handling a hurt dog, and the dangers of home treatment for a serious ailment.

> The final requirement is to know the local laws and ordinances involving dogs.

There are similar programs for Girl Scouts and 4-H members.

Local Clubs

Local dog clubs are no longer in existence just to put on a yearly dog show. Today, they are apt to be the hub of the community's involvement with pets. Dog clubs conduct educational forums with big-name speakers, stage demonstrations of canine talent in a busy mall and take dogs of various breeds to schools for class-room discussion.

The quickest way to feel accepted as a member in a club is to volunteer your services! Offer to help with something—anything—and watch your popularity (and your interest) grow.

Therapy Dogs

Once your dog has earned that essential CGC and reliably demonstrates a steady, calm temperament, you could look into what therapy dogs are doing in your area.

Therapy dogs go with their owners to visit patients at hospitals or nursing homes, generally remaining on leash but able to coax a pat from a stiffened hand, a smile from a blank face, a few words from sealed lips or a hug from someone in need of love.

Nursing homes cover a wide range of patient care. Some specialize in care of the elderly, some in the treatment of specific illnesses, some in physical therapy. Children's facilities also welcome visits from trained therapy dogs for boosting morale in their pediatric patients. Hospice care for the terminally ill and the at-home care of AIDS patients are other areas where this canine visiting is desperately needed. Therapy dog training comes first.

Your dog can make a difference in lots of lives.

There is a lot more involved than just taking your nice friendly pooch to someone's bedside. Doing therapy dog work involves your own emotional stability as well as that of your dog. But once you have met all the requirements for this work, making the rounds once a week or once a month with your therapy dog is possibly the most rewarding of all community activities.

Disaster Aid

This community service is definitely not for everyone, partly because it is time-consuming. The initial training is rigorous, and there can be no let-up in the continuing workouts, because members are on call 24 hours a day to go wherever they are needed at a moment's notice. But if you think you would like to be able to assist in a disaster, look into search-and-rescue work. The network of search-and-rescue volunteers is worldwide, and all members of the American Rescue Dog Association (ARDA) who are qualified to do this work are volunteers who train and maintain their own dogs.

Physical Aid

Most people are familiar with Seeing Eye dogs, which serve as blind people's eyes, but not with all the other work that dogs are trained to do to assist the disabled. Dogs are also specially trained to pull wheelchairs, carry school books, pick up dropped objects, open and close doors. Some also are ears for the deaf. All these assistance-trained dogs, by the way, are allowed anywhere "No Pet" signs exist (as are therapy dogs when

properly identified). Getting started in any of this fascinating work requires a background in dog training and canine behavior, but there are also volunteer jobs ranging from answering the phone to cleaning out kennels to providing a foster home for a puppy. You have only to ask.

Making the rounds with your therapy dog can be very rewarding.

part four

Beyond
the
Basics

chapter 12

Recommended Reading

Books

GENERAL

American Kennel Club (AKC). *American Kennel Club Dog Care and Training*. New York: Howell Book House, 1991.

————. *The Complete Dog Book,* 19th Edition Revised. New York: Howell Book House, 1998.

Bamberger, Michelle, DVM. *Help! The Quick Guide to First Aid for Your Dog*. New York: Howell Book House, 1995.

Carlson, Liisa, DVM, and James Giffin, MD. *Dog Owners Home Veterinary Handbook,* 3rd Edition. New York: Howell Book House, 1999.

DeBitetto, James, DVM, and Sarah Hodgson. *You & Your Puppy*. New York: Howell Book House, 2000.

Rogers Clark, Anne, and Andrew H. Brace. *The International Encyclopedia of Dogs*. New York: Howell Book House, 1995.

Vella, Bob, and Ken Leebow. *300 Incredible Things for Pet Lovers on the Internet*. Marietta, Georgia: 300 Incredible.com, 2000.

Volhard, Wendy, and Kerry Brown, DVM. *Holistic Guide for a Healthy Dog*. New York: Howell Book House, 2000.

ABOUT DOG SHOWS

Alston, George. *The Winning Edge*. New York: Howell Book House, 1992.

Hall, Lynn. *Dog Showing for Beginners*. New York: Howell Book House, 1994.

ABOUT TRAINING

Arden, Andrea. *Dog-Friendly Dog Training.* New York: Howell Book House, 1999.

Benjamin, Carol Lea. *Dog Training for Kids.* New York: Howell Book House, 1988.

————. *Dog Training in 10 Minutes.* New York: Howell Book House, 1997.

Burch, Mary, PhD, and Jon Bailey. *How Dogs Learn.* New York: Howell Book House, 1999.

Dunbar, Ian, PhD, MRCVS. *Dog Behavior: An Owner's Guide to a Happy Healthy Pet.* New York: Howell Book House, 1996.

————. *How to Teach a New Dog Old Tricks.* James & Kenneth Publishers, 1998. Order from the publisher at 2140 Shattuck Ave. #2406, Berkeley, CA 94704. (510) 658-8588.

Evans, Job Michael. *People, Pooches and Problems.* New York: Howell Book House, 2001.

Hodgson, Sarah. *Dogperfect: The User Friendly Guide to a Well Behaved Dog.* New York: Howell Book House, 1995.

New Skete Monks. *How to Be Your Dog's Best Friend.* Boston: Little Brown & Company, 1978.

Pryor, Karen. *Don't Shoot the Dog! The New Art of Teaching and Training,* Revised Edition. New York: Bantam Doubleday Dell, 1999.

Rutherford, Clarice, and David H. Neil, MRCVS. *How to Raise a Puppy You Can Live With.* Loveland, Colorado: Alpine Publications, 1982.

Volhard, Jack, and Melissa Bartlett. *What All Good Dogs Should Know: The Sensible Way to Train.* New York: Howell Book House, 1991.

ABOUT BREEDING

Finder Harris, Beth J. *Breeding a Litter: The Complete Book of Prenatal and Postnatal Care.* New York: Howell Book House, 1993.

Holst, Phyllis. *Canine Reproduction: The Breeder's Guide.* Loveland, Colorado: Alpine Publications, 1999.

Walkowicz, Chris, and Bonnie Wilcox, DVM. *Successful Dog Breeding: The Complete Handbook of Canine Midwifery.* New York: Howell Book House, 1994.

American Rescue Dog Association. *Search and Rescue Dogs.* New York: Howell Book House, 1991.

Barwig, Susan, and Stewart Hilliard. *Schutzhund.* New York: Howell Book House, 1991.

Burch, Mary. *Volunteering with Your Pet.* New York: Howell Book House, 1996.

O'Neil, Jacqueline F. *All About Agility.* New York: Howell Book House, 1999.

Vollhard, Jack and Wendy. *The Canine Good Citizen.* New York: Howell Book House, 1994.

Magazines

The AKC GAZETTE, The Official Journal for the Sport of Purebred Dogs
American Kennel Club
260 Madison Avenue
New York, NY 10016
(212) 696-8200
www.akc.org

The Bark
2810 8th Street
Berkeley, CA 94710
(510) 704-0827
www.thebark.com

Dog Fancy
Fancy Publications
3 Burroughs
Irvine, CA 92718
(949) 855-8822
www.animalnetwork.com

Dog & Kennel
Pet Publishing, Inc.
7-L Dundas Circle
Greensboro, NC 27407
(336) 292-4047
www.dogandkennel.com

Dog Watch Newsletter
P.O. Box 420235
Palm Coast, FL 32142-0235
(800) 829-5574
www.vet.cornell.edu/publicresources/dog

Dog World
Primedia
500 North Dearborn, Suite 1100
Chicago, IL 60610
(877) 224-7711
www.dogworldmag.com

Videos

"SIRIUS Puppy Training," by Ian Dunbar, PhD, MRCVS. James & Kenneth Publishers, 2140 Shattuck Ave. #2406, Berkeley, CA 94704. Order from the publisher.

"Training the Companion Dog," from Dr. Dunbar's British TV Series, James & Kenneth Publishers. (See address above.)

The American Kennel Club produces videos on every breed of dog, as well as on hunting tests, field trials and other areas of interest to purebred dog owners. For more information, write to AKC/Video Fulfillment, 5580 Centerview Dr., Suite 200, Raleigh, NC 27606. The AKC can be reached at (919) 233-9767, or visit its Web site at www.akc.org.

chapter 13

Resources

Breed Clubs and Registries

Registry organizations register purebred dogs. The American Kennel Club is the oldest and largest in the United States, and currently recognizes over 130 breeds. The United Kennel Club registers some breeds the AKC doesn't (including the American Pit Bull Terrier and the Miniature Fox Terrier), as well as many of the same breeds. The other clubs included here are for your reference; the AKC can provide you with a list of foreign registries.

Every breed recognized by the American Kennel Club has a national (parent) club. National clubs are a great source of information on your breed. You can get the name of the secretary of the club by contacting:

American Kennel Club (AKC)
260 Madison Avenue, 4th Floor
New York, NY 10016
(212) 696-8200
www.akc.org

For breeder referrals, call the customer service department in North Carolina at (919) 233-9767, or visit their Web site.

United Kennel Club (UKC)
100 East Kilgore Road
Portage, MI 49002-5584
(616) 343-9020
www.ukcdogs.com

American Rare Breed Association (ARBA)
9921 Frank Tippet Road
Cheltenham, MD 20612
(301) 868-5718
www.arba.org

155

Canadian Kennel Club (CKC)
89 Skyway Avenue
Etobicoke, Ontario
Canada M9W 6R4
(800) 250-8040
(416) 675-5511
information@ckc.ca

Health Registries

CERF
Department of Veterinary Clinical Science
School of Veterinary Medicine
Purdue University
West Lafayette, IN 47907
(765) 494-8179
yshen@vet.purdue.edu

Orthopedic Foundation for Animals (OFA)
2300 East Nifong Boulevard
Columbia, MO 65201-3856
(573) 442-0418
ofa@ofa.org
(Hip registry)

Activity Clubs

Write to the following organizations for information on the
activities they sponsor.

American Kennel Club (AKC)
260 Madison Avenue, 4th Floor
New York, NY 10016
(212) 696-8200
www.akc.org
(Conformation Shows, Obedience Trials, Field Trials and
Hunting Tests, Agility, Canine Good Citizen, Lure Coursing,
Herding, Tracking, Earthdog Tests, Coonhunting)

United Kennel Club (UKC)
100 East Kilgore Road
Portage, MI 49002-5584
(616) 343-9020
www.ukcdogs.com
(Conformation Shows, Obedience Trials, Agility, Hunting
for Various Breeds, Terrier Trials and more)

North American Flyball Association
1400 West Devon Avenue, #152
Chicago, IL 60660
www.flyball.org

Trainers

Association of Pet Dog Trainers
66 Morris Avenue, Suite 2A
Springfield, NJ 07081
(800) PET-DOGS
www.apdp.com

National Association of Dog Obedience Instructors
2286 East Steel Road
St. Johns, MI 48879
www.nadoi.org

Dog Friendly Web Sites

The following Web sites offer a variety of experiences for the dog-loving Internet surfer. Some sites present specific breed information, while others provide quizzes and questionnaires to help you decide which dog breed is the best one for you and your family. You can view photographs, research breeders and rescue organizations in your area, find out the best ways to exercise or travel with your pet or just discover more about *canis familiaris*. Enjoy!

Dog Breed Information Center
www.dogbreedinfo.com
This is a well-designed site with cute doggie graphics and easy-to-use links. Log on to donate toys to rescue organizations, post messages for like-minded dog folk, take questionnaires to discover which dog breed is best suited to your family and your home, view a plethora of canine photographs or discover the answers to frequently asked dog-care and -training questions.

Choosing the Perfect Dog
www.choosingtheperfectdog.net
Another good, all-purpose site for dog owners or dog-owner wannabes. Information is presented in a very organized manner, with helpful sidebars and links. Practical answers are given to questions such as "How do I match a dog to my lifestyle?" Or "How much time/money/stuff do I need to provide for a dog?" The site prompts visitors to think carefully about getting a dog, and to responsibly research dog breeds so that everyone involved lives happily ever after.

Good News for Pets
www.goodnewsforpets.com
This weekly digest provides interesting tidbits on all things canine related. It profiles people who are active in the dog community, provides nutrition facts, addresses legal issues

and focuses attention on how dogs are portrayed in books and on film. Visit every Monday for the "Pet Question of the Week."

Dog Advisors
www.dogadvisors.com
This is a fun site where the fancier can delve a little deeper and learn a little more about his or her favorite dog breeds. Different breeds are highlighted at various times, as are specific breeders.

United States Dog Agility Association, Inc. (USDAA)
www.usdaa.com
This USDAA is an international site that gives visitors the opportunity to find out the latest news in the world of agility training. It provides an events calendar, records titles and tournaments, defines performance standards and lists affiliated groups. "Front Page News" is updated on a weekly basis.

Canine Freestyle Federation, Inc.
www.canine-freestyle.org
Welcome to the world of Canine Freestyle—or doggie dancing, if you will. Canine freestyle is performed by dog and trainer in a ring, and all moves are choreographed to music. To learn more, visit this well-designed, comprehensive Web site. The CFF also maintains records of freestyle events and publishes a newsletter.

Pets Welcome
www.petswelcome.com
If you plan on travelling with your pet, a visit to this site is a must. The listings page offers information on over 25,000 hotels, bed & breakfasts, ski resorts, campgrounds and pet-friendly beaches. Plenty of advice and knowledge are provided for those who can't imagine leaving their pet at home.

Vet Info.com
www.vetinfo.com
If your dog is suffering from a particular ailment, you can find out more about it by visiting vetinfo.com. The format of this site is easy to use, with each disease listed in alphabetical order. To delve even deeper into your pet's health, you might subscribe to *Vetinfo Digest* for its "Ask Dr. Mike" Segment.